THE GORDON BENNETT GUARANTEE

Nobody, following my methods, will ever
  (a) Be taken unawares by the unexpected event.
  (b) Go into business unprepared for the worst.
  (c) Be invited to address the annual meeting of the Institute of Directors.

I, Gordon Bennett, will take you through each painful step to the top, and at the top of the business world today stands the Management Consultant, the Oracle, the Supremo, whose word is Truth, and whose fee is Exorbitant.

TO JULIE

HOW TO TRY HARD IN BUSINESS WITHOUT REALLY SUCCEEDING

by Charles Grahame

Everyone said that it couldn't be done,
But he gritted his teeth and set to it—
And he tackled the job that couldn't be done,
And he couldn't do it.

ICARUS

ST. MARTIN'S PRESS
NEW YORK

Copyright © 1975 by George Allen & Unwin Ltd.
For information, write: St. Martin's Press,
175 Fifth Avenue, New York, N.Y. 10010
Manufactured in the United States of America

Library of Congress Cataloging in Publication Data

Grahame, Charles.
    How to try hard in business without really
succeeding.

    1. Business.   2. Success.   I. Title.
HF5351.G66   1982   650.1'0207   81-14495
ISBN 0-312-39582-5   AACR2

Introduction

Starting with £100, Mr A, by a series of shrewd investments on the stock market, increased his capital to £2,000 in nine months. With this money he bought a half share in an ailing engineering company, and within three years had built the business into a thriving concern, employing 400, with an annual turnover of £50 million.

This book is not meant for Mr A.

Neither is it meant for Mr B, who, penniless at the age of twenty-one, obtained a job as a filing clerk with a film company, and at twenty-six was financial director and a millionaire in his own right.

Nor yet Mr C, who, with his wartime gratuity purchased a derelict house, rebuilt it with his own hands, sold it for £1,500, bought six more derelict houses, and now heads a £150 million property empire.

Mr A would develop ulcers reading this book. Mr B, who already has ulcers, would have a stroke. Mr C never learned to read.

No, this book is for Mr Y, who started his business career with £250 from an endowment policy, and at the age of thirty-nine has an overdraft of £149. Also Mr Z, who left school with absolutely nothing, and thirty years later has increased his fortune to a £5 Premium Bond and a ticket in the Irish Sweep.

You are not alone, Messrs Y and Z.

Chapter 1

A Short Summary of Business Books

There have been many good books written about business, and they make it seem so simple that there is, one would imagine, no excuse for anyone to fail. The fact remains that no one has ever made a fortune from reading a business book, and the reason is that fortunes are invariably created through the lucky accident. Certainly, the man who can wade through these volumes of wisdom will, if he can stay awake, become a better clerk or salesman, and eventually make chief clerk or sales manager, but his chances of making his million are slightly less than winning the football pools in a jackpot week.

The autobiographies of millionaires, who cannot resist putting their cleverness into print, tend to confirm this theory. Sir Frazer McIsaacs, in *My First Two Million* (Hairey & Spottiface, £2·50) claims to have worked twenty hours a day, seven days a week, and then he married an heiress. How he met an heiress in the four hours left to him each day he does not explain, although this information alone would be worth the cost of his book.

Mr Gall Petty, in *Oil I Want Is a Living* (Hoxton University Press, £3·75) is the son of a poor Texan farmer, who left his log cabin one day to go and build a bigger and better latrine at the end of his cabbage patch. Mr Petty just took it from there.

In *Success with a Bang* (Cannon & Fodder, £4·50), Baron Fritz von Katzkrapp frankly admits that business was far from good until his over-enthusiastic salesman in Sarajevo tried to demonstrate the company's latest product to the Archduke Franz Ferdinand. Sales have never stopped booming.

All this information is worse than useless to the budding business-man. What he needs is a solidly practical book of advice backed by experience, and written by one of the world's great businessmen who has the courage to admit the occasional error, and the strength to overcome it.

The Gordon Bennett Guarantee

Nobody, following my methods, will ever

    (*a*) Be taken unawares by the unexpected event.
    (*b*) Go into business unprepared for the worst.

(*c*) Be invited to address the annual meeting of the Institute of Directors.

I, Gordon Bennett, will take you through each painful step to the top, and at the top of the business world today stands the Management Consultant, the Oracle, the Supremo, whose word is Truth, and whose fee is Exorbitant.

Chapter 2

Problems in Management Consultancy. Price Structurisation and Independent Adjustable Variants Using Fibre Tip Syndromatic Technique

It is not difficult to become a successful Management Consultant, providing you follow one cardinal rule: never actually DO anything. You may talk indefinitely; give advice, make recommendations, recommend redundancies; hold meetings, look wise, even write the odd report, but never, never lay your hand to a job of work, because sure as fate they will find you out.

When I lived in Amsterdam, one of the companies which sought my services as a consultant was a business specialising in selling hair-pieces to men. They had a shop in the centre of the city, and I lived in the top floor flat for two crowded years. The shop manager was a sharp, deeply amoral salesman called Albert, and he and I whiled away many a sleepy afternoon sitting by the first floor window quietly watching the students rioting and the hippies scratching, and noting with satisfaction the great number of solid Dutch burghers with bald heads.

One day, Albert jumped to his feet and pointed to a passer-by who was apparently balancing a dead ginger cat on his head.

'What a terrible wig that man is wearing', Albert said. 'I will sell him a new one.' He galloped downstairs, and I followed, anxious to see a master salesman at work. The passer-by had stopped to look in our window, and Albert opened the door, smiling like a shark, and said conversationally, 'Good afternoon, meneer, you are wearing a terrible wig.'

'I know', the man said sadly. 'You sold it to me two months ago.'

A lesser man than Albert would have flinched and run away, and that is what I did. Straight up to the kitchen I went to make myself a nice strong cup of tea. Meanwhile Albert somehow enticed the man into the shop, and soon had him settled in a chair in the manager's office. From the kitchen I peered through the hatch, and although my Dutch was not good enough to follow the conversation, I could tell that Albert was well on the way to another sale. Such a salesman makes a consultant's job easy, I thought, good old Albert, but then a cold shiver ran through me as I heard Albert say, 'I will bring the barber from Stoke-on-Trent to examine you.' I dashed up to my bedroom, and just failed to lock the door in time. Albert came in grinning, carrying a white coat.

'I do not intend to examine anyone's head', I said. 'I am not a barber, and I am certainly not from Stoke-on-Trent. I am a Management Consultant, and I have been hired by your company at a substantial fee—which, incidentally, I have not yet received—and anyway, why Stoke-on-Trent?'

'It is such a funny name', said Albert. 'Come on, put the coat on and help me.'

'How can I help you?' I protested. 'I know nothing about wigs, except how much they cost to make, and how much you sell them for, and how much commission you earn.'

'Then', said Albert, 'you know all there is that is worth knowing. The man is being difficult, and you will make it easy because he can speak English to you, and all Dutchmen like to practise their English with a real Englishman.'

I considered it. Perhaps it would help me. All business experience is useful to a Management Consultant.

'Also,' said Albert, 'I will buy you dinner tonight at Schiller's if we make the sale.'

I took the coat. It belonged to one of the smaller girls, and while I struggled into it Albert explained, 'Men with bald heads do not trust managers or consultants, but everyone trusts barbers. Who knows more about hair, barbers or Management Consultants?' I saw the logic of this, but who would trust a man in a white coat which ended just below his waist, with sleeves midway between wrist and elbow? Also, I could only do up one button. I supposed I looked as much like a barber from Stoke-on-Trent as I ever would, and I followed Albert downstairs with grave misgivings. The Institute of Management Consultants would have struck me off on the spot.

'Meneer van Mol,' said Albert, 'this is meneer Gordon Bennett, the barber from Stoke-on-Trent.'

'*Goede middag, meneer*', I said in perfect Dutch.

'You do not speak Hollands, then', said meneer van Mol in perfect English. I shrugged, wondering what I had actually said.

'It is a hard language, too hard for an Englishman', said van Mol, adding, 'I have been to Weston-super-Mare.'

'Good heavens!', I said, wonder in my voice. 'What a coincidence!'

'Is near Stoke-on-Trent, yes?'

'Is very near', I said. I was not in the mood for geography.

Albert said, 'I want you to examine meneer van Mol's head for a very special hair-piece.' He handed me a comb, and taking it between finger and thumb I lightly touched van Mol's head with it.

'Yes', I said. 'I think we can manage that.'

'Perhaps', said Albert, standing behind van Mol, 'we should start—here.' He bent over the bald defenceless head and made a mark on it with his marking pen. He stood back, and I saw that he had written across the shiny pate, '2,000'. I was shocked. Two thousand guilders, about £225, was a bit stiff, even for us. Taking from the desk a fibre tipped pen, I said, 'You mean, like—this?' and crossed out the '2,000' and wrote 'too much'. Albert held his chin in his fingers thoughtfully where van Mol could see him, then bent forward over the head again.

'Do you not think, meneer Bennett, that we should do—this?' He wrote '1,750'. With a perfectly straight face, I crossed out the '1,750' and wrote, '1,600'. Then confidence oozing, I said, 'A natural parting—here', and wrote around the perimeter of the head, '*Sole meunière* at Schiller's'. Albert, closing the sale as he had been taught, said, 'Yes meneer van Mol, we can make you a perfect hair-piece: finest north European hair guaranteed not to fade, natural parting, patented breathing lining, for 1,600 guilders', and wrote on the small part of van Mol's scalp that was still available, 'You buy the *vino*'. He then took a large jar of cream from a cupboard, and smeared the contents thickly over van Mol's head, and wiped it off. All the writing that Albert had done with his marking pen had disappeared, but my fibre tipped comments remained as bright and clear as a neon sign. My heart stopped beating, and Albert stood there unable to believe his eyes, lost for words for the first time in his life. He tried again, but the writing was immovable. We looked at each other in panic. Albert was the first to recover.

'Meneer', he said, 'I will take measurements.' Swiftly he covered the head with a sheet of plastic, and fastened it with sticky tape. 'I will be back soon', he said, and we both retreated to the kitchen.

'You fool', Albert said. 'Why did you use that pen?'

'It's your fault', I said. 'I've never written on a head before.'

We searched the kitchen for materials which might clean the writing from poor van Mol's head. Albert tried butter. It only made the bald head shine like a billiard ball. I tried vinegar. Van Mol gave a chirp of protest, but I was in no state to listen to him. Vinegar does not remove ink marks from bald heads. Albert took something from the fridge. 'You can't use that,' I protested, 'it cost six guilders', but he had gone with my cream cheese with herbs. 'This is a special treatment', he told a now-alarmed van Mol, 'to strengthen the hair roots.'

'It smells like cheese', van Mol said.

I ran upstairs to my bathroom and collected a nailbrush and some detergent, and at the same time checked my airline ticket, just in case. Albert was massaging the cheese vigorously into van Mol's head, and I took over and mixed the detergent with the cheese and began to scrub with the brush. The smell was appalling.

'In Stoke-on-Trent', I said, 'everyone treats his hair with this special ointment. Nowhere in the world is there such healthy hair as in Stoke-on-Trent, not Weston-super-Mare, not Ashby-de-la-Zouche, not . . .' I realised I was rambling. I wiped the disgusting concoction off, and van Mol's head had changed colour. It was bright pink. Clearly visible were the words—'too much', '1,600', and '*Sole meunière* at Schiller's'. If the worst came to the worst, perhaps I could get an advertising fee from meneer Schiller.

Albert disappeared, to enter almost immediately, desperation in his eyes and my liver sausage and mayonnaise in his hands, and as he set to work I went up to my room again to seek inspiration. I saw my after-shave lotion and grabbed it. Van Mol was beginning to shout at Albert and I pushed him away, wiped the head clean and poured on my expensive after-shave.

'*Godverdomme*!' roared van Mol, leaping a good twelve inches from his chair and clutching his scalp. 'What you do to me? Is this how you treat your clients in Weston-super-Mare? My poor nut is all fire!'

'For true beauty,' I murmured, 'a certain discomfort must be endured.' I had regained my confidence, because the after-shave had done the trick. Van Mol's head was scarlet and patchy, but it was as clear and clean as a baby's.

The sale was not made. Meneer van Mol left, his remaining wispy black hair once again covered by his ginger wig. He was bellowing what I took to be threats of personal violence against Albert and me, but I was not worried; Management Consultants are used to threats of personal violence.

I insisted on Albert taking me to dinner, though. After all, he had used up all my food.

Chapter 3

Of course it took many years of study and experience before I became a Management Consultant. I started my working life with only one aim: a fortune in the quickest possible time. If I had my life over again, I should choose a different business, like banking, or property developing, or scrap metal, or selling matches, or, in fact, anything other than catering. I would be quite happy to leave catering to Sir Charles Forte, who seems to have the knack.

When Stan and I were demobbed from the RAF we decided to open a chain of restaurants. Not all at once, but one or two a year until we had one in every British city with a population exceeding 95,000. Corporate planning, this is known as in the Management Consultancy game. Many hours were spent in discussing whether Grimsby or Halifax should be included, both of which had fluctuating populations around the critical mark. We finally selected Grimsby, after a close study of statistics indicated a gradual increase there, as against a decided yet understandable trend by Halifaxonians to get the hell out.

Our plans met an unforeseen setback. The Ministry of Food refused to give us a licence. In vain we haunted the authorities, using threats, eloquence and pathos. We drew the last ounce of advantage from our position as ex-servicemen, on one occasion going so far as to put a bloodstained bandage around Stan's head and borrowing a young child from a neighbour to lead him faltering into the interview room, but the incorruptible ministry held firm.

'When food rationing ends,' we were told, 'you will not need a licence.' Since the end of food rationing seemed as likely as the abolition of income tax, we drew no comfort from this; but there was another way into catering. We could buy an existing business and take over the licence.

Thus our first valuable lesson in business, nay, in life, was learned: Try, strive, fight for what you want with every fibre of your being, and if you fail, as you probably will, buy it.

Capital Expenditure in Peripatetic Enterprise

Now came our second setback. The prices of established restaurants were astronomical. We went rapidly down the scale: cafés, snack-bars, pull-ins, and once we inspected an eel and pie shop, but Stan was smitten by an attack of nausea when he glimpsed the enamel bowls of green jelly. Eventually we gave up the hunt, but at this lowest ebb I saw an advertisement which rekindled the flame.

'Stan,' I said, 'there's a mobile canteen advertised here. It's only £2,500, o.n.o., s.a.v., t/o £200 p.w.'

'We don't want it', he said.

'Licensed', I continued, 'for race meetings.'

'Where is it?' Stan said, a sudden gleam in his eye.

It was near the Elephant and Castle, in deepest south London, and it was owned by a large, fat cockney with the unlikely name of Tom Smith. Sitting in his front-room, we listened with mounting enthusiasm as he recounted his adventures and financial successes.

'Now, at Alexander Park last month', Tom told us, 'I made a killing. Took twenty quid before the first race. 'Ad to send ma for another six loaves, in a taxi, wasn't it ma?'

Ma, a frail old lady, smiled weakly.

'Quickly opened two tins of salmon, made the lot up into sandwiches, sold out by 'alf three, thirty-five nikker in the drawer, eh ma?'

'Excuse me,' I said, 'I don't know much about catering, but surely you need more than two tins of salmon for six loaves?'

'They was big tins', Tom said. 'It's just one of the tricks of the trade, son, and there's no one knows more about the mobile lark than Tom Smith, right ma?'

'If you make so much money,' I asked, 'why are you selling the canteen?'

'Well, it's me old ma, ennit?' Tom said, trying unsuccessfully to look tender. 'She keeps getting these heart attacks, don't she. Last week at Plumpton I thought she was goin' to snuff it. Collapsed in the back, let the urn run dry, worst thing you can do in this business. I 'ad a queue of fifty punters lined up, and by the time I finished serving them, all by meself, she was bright blue in the face. It's not fair on me, I can't do everythin' on me tod, can I?'

Ma, at that moment, was looking a bit blue, and her breathing was uneven, and I accepted Tom's explanation without further questions.

When Tom eventually showed us the mobile canteen, we had a bit of a shock. It was a shabby cream Chevrolet which might have fetched two hundred pounds. The equipment consisted of an urn, several chipped cups without saucers, and two leaden teaspoons tied to the counter with string. Our spirits sank, and Tom saw our faces.

'Look boys, you're not paying two and a half grand for a van and a couple of spoons. You're buying the licence, which is worth solid gold, and a site on every race-course in the country. And I'll tell you what I'll do. I'll take you with me to Chester tomorrow, there's a three-day meeting there, an' you can see for yourselves 'ow much money there is in this game.'

This was a fair offer, which we accepted, and as we walked away Stan said, 'I suppose we must buy it, if only to save ma's life.'

Quality Control and the Industrial Econ/Ratio in Consumer Non-Durables

What we should have done was to disappear quietly from the lives of Tom Smith and his poor mother, but the idea of three days at the races was too appealing, so at six o'clock next morning we presented ourselves at Tom's house, and soon we were on our way north. Tom sang all the way, ma groaned, Stan studied the Chester race card and I dozed. The van was loaded with bread, rolls, and bottles of milk, and on our arrival at Chester Tom drove around until he found a space near the entrance of the race-course, and wedged the van in securely. Two minutes later another canteen drove up, and the driver said that we were in his pitch, whereupon Tom said hard luck mate. The driver dismounted aggressively, apparently intent upon fisticuffs, but when he saw Stan and me standing shoulder to shoulder with Tom, he retreated, muttering threats. I was bucked. I had never frightened anyone before.

We began, under Tom's tuition, to cut rolls, grate cheese and boil eggs, and I was sent to search for water for the urn. It was all delightfully primitive, and I felt like a boy scout at his first camp. Then Tom showed me the salmon trick. He took a loaf of bread and cut off all the crusts. The bread was then cut into pieces and placed in a large bowl, and a mixture of vinegar and water poured over it, and then a tin of fish was added. The fish was either very anaemic salmon or slightly sunburnt cod, and the resultant mess looked exceptionally unappetising.

'Now', said Tom, 'for the Piece of Resistance', and he produced a tiny bottle of cochineal colouring and added a few drops. 'Give that a good mashing, son,' he said, 'and you've got enough Grade One salmon to make up a hundred sandwiches at one and a tanner each.'

Stan, who was on the mundane task of making cheese rolls, shot me an envious glance. 'There'll be no holding you after this', he said sourly. 'Today the loaves and fishes, tomorrow walking on the water.'

Actually, I was not feeling very happy as I mashed my mixture. This was so far removed from my original vision of the Mirabelle or the Caprice. '*Sole bonne femme*', I sighed aloud, as I removed a large piece of black skin from my bowl.

'What's that you said?' asked Tom, putting the skin back.

'I just said "*Sole bonne femme*" ', I said.

'Forget about women', Tom said. 'Keep your mind on your work.'

Business was terrific during the only three hot days of that year. Every half hour Tom removed the notes from the cash drawer and stuffed them in his hip pocket, and at the end of each day he triumphantly counted them and solemnly presented Stan and me with one pound each as our wages. 'I know you don't need the money, boys', he said. 'This is just for cigarettes.'

At the end of the third day the canteen had taken £184. Stock had cost £32. Gross profit, £152. Net profit, after deducting petrol, lodgings, Calor gas and our wages, a minimum of £130. For three days work! Driving back to London, Stan and I worked it out, while Tom sang dirty songs and ma turned grey and blue alternately. If we worked seven days a week, as we would, of course, that made a net profit of over £300 a week! A fortune!

The Advisability of Second Opinions. The Approach to Possible Financial Sources

Next morning, on an impulse, I telephoned my rich uncle.

'Uncle,' I said, 'I am thinking of buying a business.'

I could almost hear the wheels turning in his brain as he thought, 'This is going to cost me if I'm not very careful.' Finally he said, slowly, 'What business?'

'Well,' I said, 'it's a catering business.'

'What sort of catering business?'

'A mobile catering business,' I said. 'I want your opinion.'

'My opinion?' he said, relieved. 'My opinion is, "forget it".'

'But uncle,' I said, 'it's a good business, and it's only £2,500.'

'Have you got £2,500?'

'No,' I said. 'But I have a partner.'

'Does he have £2,500?'

'No.'

'Forget it,' my uncle said.

Eventually I persuaded him to come with me to meet Tom Smith and see the canteen. He called for me in his Bentley, and on the way I told him all about it, the trip to Chester, the phenomenal takings, the huge profit. He drove in gloomy silence.

'Who took the money?' he asked at last.

'Tom Smith, of course', I said.

'How do you know that Mr Smith did not add £50 to the takings?' he asked. 'How do you know that the stock did not cost more than Mr Smith told you? What proof have you that Mr Smith did not invent all the figures?'

'Tom Smith would not do that!' I said, aghast.

'Why not?' my uncle asked. 'I would, if I was dealing with a mug.'

'And what', went on my rich uncle, 'makes you think that your expensive education has fitted you to become the proprietor of a . . . a coffee stall?'

'It's not a coffee stall,' I protested, 'it's a mobile canteen, licensed for race meetings.'

Tom Smith met us at the garage. He was disturbed when he saw my uncle. 'Morning guvnor', he said, and touched his forelock. My uncle ignored him, walked once round the van, kicking each tyre in turn, and returned to the Bentley.

'Get in', he said to me.

I was subdued on the return journey. Uncle was also subdued.

'I am disappointed in you', he said. 'You seem to have no business sense and no common sense. Frankly, I do not know what to do about you. Will you take my advice?'

It was the only thing he had ever given me, so I listened.

'Don't you ever give another thought to purchasing that contraption.'

He never spoke to me again, because the following day we bought it.

Practical Negotiation between Principals

'In your advertisement', I said to Tom, 'it says £2,500 or near offer.'

'That's right', Tom said.

'Would you call £1,500 a near offer?' I asked.

'I would call £1,500 a bleed'n ridiculous offer', Tom said equably.

'In your hand, today, in used one pound notes', I said quietly.

'Not in bleed'n gold dust, mate', Tom said, equally quietly.

'You see,' Stan said brightly, 'we haven't got £2,500.'

We both rounded on him angrily. He had destroyed my plan, and the mood I had tried to create of two ice-cold, razor-sharp brains fencing and probing. I had seen it done long ago, in a film about the Rothschilds.

Tom said, 'If you cheeky gits 'ave been 'aving me on. . . .'

This also damaged the Rothschild image, which ma finally smashed beyond redemption by bringing in some bottles of brown ale and three packets of potato crisps.

Finally, we made an unbelievably good deal. We agreed to pay the full £2,500, half in cash at once, and the remainder at the rate of 50 per cent of our net profits, weekly.

At four o'clock in the afternoon, having paid £1,250 and signed an agreement, we were in business. We left the van with Tom temporarily, because neither Stan nor I had the nerve to drive it, and we took a taxi to Stan's house. We were intoxicated by the thought of £300 profit a week, and the first thing Stan did on arriving home was to make a telephone call.

'Who you phoning, Stan?' I asked.

'Mr Simmins, at the garage. I'm ordering a Riley 2½ litre', Stan said.

'Order one for me too, Stan,' I said, 'in bronze.'

The Marketing of Comestible Alternates—Hippodromatic Outlets

There were several reasons why we did not make money. First of all, although our licence permitted us to sell refreshments at race-meetings, most race-course authorities did not, preferring to make their own catering arrangements for the precious few who attend the average race track. Even at an important meeting, where the attendance ran into many thousands, and we were given a pitch in a good position, the competition was so great that it was rarely possible to take more than fifteen pounds a day. The sixty-odd pounds daily that we took at Chester, we discovered all too late, was impossible. We had been cheated. Had we spent one single week on market research before we bought the canteen we should have saved a lot of money.

Our one great extravagance was our hired help. Ted was a middle-aged Londoner, narrow and shrewd, and we met him in a pub.

'You boys don't know how to run a gaff like this', he assured us when we showed him the canteen. 'You need someone a bit rough and ready, who knows how to chat up the cops, and who to drop a few bob to for a decent pitch.'

The Chevrolet van had a certain malevolence, which we never cured. The windscreen wipers worked well, except when it rained, and then they went faster and faster until they flew off. Another of the van's favourite tricks, which became endearing in time, was always played when we were going downhill: its bonnet flaps would raise simultaneously, each side of the engine, and we would flutter along like some monstrous bird. On such occasions we would cheer, and for some unremembered reason, fire imaginary rifles at passers-by. But the most unattractive fault, which we were quite unable to remedy, was the leaking windscreen, and Stan, who had become the permanent driver, suffered greatly. Whenever it rained, water poured in at a position immediately above his knee, and it was my job on these occasions to hold a teapot over his lap and catch the water through the spout. Any efficiency expert could have told us that this was a most inadequate method of dealing with the trouble, but it quickly became a tradition, and I would never have dreamed of catching the raindrops in any other way, nor would Stan have allowed it.

The Marketing of Comestible Alternatives—Up-Trading

The Epsom Derby meeting was the highlight of the year, but every canteen in Great Britain was there. At our evening conference, Ted made a suggestion.

'We must do something that the others don't do', he said. 'All these canteens, they treat their customers like pigs. Look at us, two dirty teaspoons tied to the counter. We should give them a bit of luxury. Let's get a couple of dozen teaspoons, good ones, chrome, and treat the clients like human beings.'

'But Ted,' I said, 'we do not supply saucers. Where would they put their spoons?'

'Anyway,' said Stan, 'I always give them a good stir after I put the sugar in.'

'And that's another thing', Ted said. 'Why not let them help themselves to sugar? Put a big notice up, "Help Yourselves to Sugar". That'll fetch them.'

Sugar at that time was still rationed, and Ted's idea was truly revolutionary.

'Good management thinking, Ted', Stan said.

Next day we set the mobile catering industry in a ferment. People could not believe their eyes. 'Help ourselves?', they said. 'Are you sure? How many can we have?' The older folk in particular were delighted. Watching us slyly, they shovelled sugar into their tea in vast quantities, and stirred with shiny new spoons. We were showered with compliments.

At the end of the day we did some research. We found that we had sold no more teas than usual. We had, however, used a week's ration of sugar, and we had also lost twenty-four chrome teaspoons.

Directional Flexibility in Neo-Consumer Exploration. Agencies of Collection in Quadrate Motive Operations

The end came, to our relief, at the end of a long, wet summer. We had been flitting about the country, occasionally hitting a stroke of

23

luck and breaking even, but we grew tired of race-meetings and long hours on the road. One of Ted's friends was going hopping, and suggested that we try our luck there. Each year there was a migration of south Londoners to the hopfields of Kent, and for a month entire families lived in huts, gathering the hop harvest by day and whooping it up by night. We knew that it was against the terms of our licence to sell refreshments at the hopfields, but we no longer cared for such niceties.

Tom Smith had been troublesome, demanding money under our agreement. He had a point, there is no denying it. Of the £1,250 we owed him, we had repaid precisely £27, and although he had no legal recourse, because we never made a net profit, he had resorted to threats of personal injury. To me, a threat of personal injury carries far more influence than any writ, and our last conversation with Tom had verged on the dangerous.

'You 'eard of the Elephant mob?' he asked darkly.

'No, Tom, I don't think I have', I said civilly. 'I have heard of the Leopard men of central Africa. They wear leopard masks and skins, and attach claws to their hands, don't they? The *News of the World* prints stories about them every two years.'

'The Elephant mob ain't in Africa, son. They're 'ere, at the Elephant and Castle. And they don't wear claws, they carry chivs. I am very pally with some of the Elephant mob. They'll always do Tom Smith a favour.'

'Are you suggesting that we take the canteen to one of their lodge meetings?' I asked. 'What a good idea, Tom.'

'No, I ain't suggesting that at all, son', Tom said. 'They just don't like to see one of their mates get taken, that's all.'

'There is no point in threatening us, Tom', I said. 'We have friends in the Balls Pond Road mob, up at Dalston. You would be surprised what they carry in their hands.'

The threats did in fact worry us. Stan and me against the Elephant mob was an unfair contest, and we began to think seriously about retirement. We advertised the canteen for sale, but discovered that we did not own a particularly desirable business. The old Chevrolet's life was drifting peacefully towards its close, and we could certainly not afford a new vehicle.

The relatively short journey to the hopfields was a far more practical proposition than our long and arduous trips to far flung race-courses, so we found ourselves a pitch in the forecourt of a pub situated in the centre of the hopping country, and, incredibly, began to make a profit.

The Emotional Factor in Partnership. The Importance of Accurate Valuation in Stock Exchange Deals

It was Stan's tender heart which ended it all. His generosity with our meagre takings in the past had resulted in a collection of useless articles accumulating in the cupboard under the counter. People used to approach him on race-courses with tragic tales of misfortune—and there is nowhere on earth where you will find more tales of tragic misfortune than on a race-course—and say, 'Look, guv, someone's nicked my wallet, and I'm skint. Can you lend us a couple of quid to get home? I'll give it back tomorrow, and you can keep my raincoat [or watch, or lighter] as security', and Stan would hand over the money, and the stranger would never be seen again.

At the hopfields, whenever it was his turn to go to the pub to refill our milk churn, in which we kept our water supply, one of us had to go looking for him, and invariably he was discovered in the centre of a row of old ladies, arms linked, dancing the traditional 'Knees Up Mother Brown'.

'Stan,' I remonstrated, 'what sort of businessman are you? Do you think that Henry Ford or Gulbenkian ever deserted their businesses for a knees-up?'

'You're only jealous', Stan said, 'because they won't dance with you.'

One afternoon, during a quiet spell, Ted and I went for a short stroll, and when we returned I looked at Stan's face and I knew he had been up to something. I went straight to the drawer to check the money, and saw with relief that it was still there. I checked the inventory under the counter, and it was unchanged: three decrepit raincoats, a box containing two broken watches, three lighters, a metal cigarette case, and a ring so obviously made of lead that only my partner would have accepted the owner's word that it was platinum.

'Stan,' I said to him patiently at the time, 'if you can write with it, it is not platinum. And if the stone, when you look into it, has a picture of a naked lady, it is almost certainly not a diamond.' I was happy to see that no more treasures had been added.

'What have you done, Stan?' I said.

'Nothing at all', he swore, 'except. . . .'

'Oh my God', I said.

'Look, all I did was promise to give a lift to someone', Stan said. 'A poor old man, you know him, the old costermonger who helps the pickers take their luggage to the station on his horse and cart. He has to get back to London tonight. I said we would drop him off near Hackney.'

'Hackney is miles out of our way,' I complained, 'and the old man smells. Honestly, Stan, you can't be left on your own.'

At nine o'clock that evening we had packed everything away, and I sat fuming, waiting for our passenger to arrive.

'Five minutes I'll give him,' I said, 'just five minutes, and if he's not here we're leaving.' Then he arrived, an old man in a muffler and flat cap, leading his horse.

'Where are you leaving the horse?' I said. 'Hurry up, we're late.'

'Leaving the 'orse?' the old man said. 'Why, 'e's coming, ain't 'e. Your gaffer said.'

'What!' I gasped. Stan said, 'I said nothing about a horse. You asked me for a lift, but you didn't say anything about your horse.'

'Well, I'm not riding anywhere with a horse,' Ted said, 'and that's final.'

'No one is riding anywhere with a horse', I said calmly. 'It was a misunderstanding. This is a canteen, not a horsebox. Leave him in a field somewhere until tomorrow.'

'But 'e said we could come', the old man said, near to tears. 'Your gaffer there, 'e said "Sure, I'll drop you orf near 'ackney", you ask 'im. That's right, ain't it guv'nor?'

'Not with your bloody horse', Stan shouted. 'You old fool, how can you get a horse in here?'

'You haven't', I said, as a sudden thought struck me, 'brought your cart as well, have you?'

'No, of course not', the old man said. 'That's the trouble. One of me mates wiv a lorry took me cart back this afternoon. I mean, the 'ole thing was because if I go back on the 'orse and cart it takes me so long, because the 'orse is getting on now, she's over twenty-five years old and she keeps stopping, and it was raining, and it would of taken us near a day and night to get back to 'ackney, so when your gaffer there said 'e'd give us a lift, I sent the cart on a'ead sort of, see?'

'I suppose', Stan said, 'we couldn't. . . .'

'No, we couldn't', I said. 'You're mad, Stan. Suppose the horse starts kicking, he could kill us all. And if we were stopped by the law, we would lose our licence so fast. . . .'

'She's only a little 'orse', the old man said. 'She's ever so gentle, she wouldn't kick or be no trouble. I'd sit by 'er, and 'old 'er 'ead all the time, I would. You wouldn't know she was there, honest. Do us a favour, mates.'

'She is very little', Stan said. 'I've never seen a smaller horse ever, have you Ted?'

'Don't ask me,' Ted snarled, 'don't any one ask me anything. It's not my canteen, you do what you like with it, but don't ask me what

I think because I'll tell you now, I think you are stone bonkers, the lot of you.'

'She wouldn't get through the back door, anyway', I said.

'Let's see', Stan said.

She could get through, just. We had to stand behind her and push, and when her front legs were in, we had to lift her back legs up, but it was surprisingly easy. The old man said she should have travelled the other way round, facing the rear, but Stan put his foot down and said he was not going to drive with his head between the mare's back legs.

It was a miserable journey. Stan drove, I sat beside him holding the teapot over his knees to catch the rain, the old man stood behind me holding the horse's head, the mare stood trembling, long strings of slobber hanging from her mouth, and Ted sat on the counter at the back, his usual place, muttering only the occasional word when the mare swished her tail in his face.

Considering the weather and the internal conditions, we made good time, and we were crossing the darkest part of Blackheath when there was a sudden earsplitting sound. For a moment I thought we had hit something, but the noise, of a gigantic rainstorm, was inside the van.

Stan shouted, 'The urn! The bloody horse has turned the urn on! Turn it off! The urn, Ted! It is the urn! Is it the urn? Christ, let it be the urn!'

It was not the urn.

A nightmare followed. The noise went on and on and on. Steam began to fill the van, and Stan slammed the brakes on. The horse was forced forward, and its slobbery mouth took Stan in the back of the neck. I was in some kind of cataleptic trance, and the brimming teapot slipped from my fingers into Stan's lap.

'Stop it, you old fool,' Stan sobbed at the old man, 'it's your horse, stop it!'

'It will stop soon, guv'nor, it always does stop', the old man gibbered. 'Any minute now it'll stop, you wait.'

An appalling smell now added to our panic. The horse's head was jammed between Stan and me, and we were both being pushed against the windscreen, unable to move. My feet were suddenly wet and warm.

As quickly as it started, the terrible noise ceased. The horse retreated, releasing me, and I stood up and switched on the interior light. Dimly through the steam I could see Ted shaking his trouser legs, and uttering unbelievable oaths. He must have caught the full force.

Then there was a deathly silence, broken only by the sound of softly running water. There was nothing to say.

27

Ted broke the silence. 'The cheese rolls are done for', he said.

'No, no!' the old man said hoarsely. 'They'll be all right. I'll give them a wipe over.'

We held an immediate discussion, with our legs held high. The old man said, 'She never done this before. She won't do it again tonight, she never goes twice.'

I said, 'Open all the doors and let it all run out. Then we can mop up the rest with the old raincoats.'

Ted said, 'This is me lot. I'm off. I'll have me cards in the morning.'

Stan, who had suffered most, made a statement that was neither logical, helpful nor possible.

We dropped the old man at Hackney and Ted at his home. The canteen was put in its garage, and Stan and I sat down on the curb and howled.

How to Finish

We never used the canteen again. In the morning we telephoned Tom Smith and told him we were giving up the business, and would he like to give us our money back. He was speechless. Well, we said, give us half back. He laughed. Well, goodbye then, we said.

Wait, he said, he could give us £150. We were speechless.

After alternate offers and attacks of speechlessness, we agreed to take £350. We had lost £900 in less than a year, and we were happy.

When we opened the doors of the canteen the stench knocked us backwards. We hosed it down for an hour, then poured bottles of disinfectant everywhere. Finally we emptied a whole bottle of Stan's sister's 'Jolie Madame' into each corner and cranny.

We drove to Tom's house and returned his canteen. He was glad to see it again, but ma looked unhappy. Tom opened the driver's door and screwed up his nose. 'Blimey!' he said. 'What have you done to it? It stinks like an Algerian brothel.' He sniffed again twice, like a connoisseur of fine wine. 'What a horse has pissed in', he added.

Back at Stan's, we shared out the money, weak with relief. Then Stan began to telephone.

'Who are you phoning, Stan?' I asked.

'Mr Simmins, at the garage', he said. 'I'm cancelling my Riley 2½ litre.'

'Cancel mine too, Stan', I said.

Chapter 4

Starting Again. Techniques of Oral Marketing. The
Personality/Progress Inverse Ratio

On the basis of my long experience in the food business, I obtained
a job with an old established firm of food importers in the City. The
boss, Mr Quagga, was a friendly old man.

'We expect great things of you', he told me on my first morning.
'I have received a first-class reference from your previous employer.'

I knew it was a good one. Stan wrote it.

'The way we operate here is simple', Mr Quagga went on. 'I
purchase consignments of canned foods and your two colleagues,
Mr Robinson and Mr Fieldman, sell them to wholesalers throughout
the country. You will join them, and when you have had some
experience of selling, I have interesting plans for expansion in which
you will play a major part.'

I thanked him and assured him that his expansion policy was safe
in my hands, and then went in to join my fellow salesmen.

For two days I listened to them. Entirely on the telephone, they
sold cases of West Indian grapefruit, Australian pineapples, Polish
ham and Italian tomatoes. As soon as a sale was made, details were
passed through to the despatch department and instructions were
issued to the wharves where to send the goods. Thus, we never saw
any of the food we sold, nor tasted it, and we never met any of our
customers.

It was ridiculously easy. Then, for my first solo, I was given a
shipment of Naples plum peeled tomatoes to dispose of, and I could
not sell them.

'I think', said Mr Robinson, 'that your telephone technique needs
sharpening up. Listen to me for a bit.'

He called a Nottingham wholesaler. 'Hello, Mr Rawtenstal,' he
said, 'it's old Robinson of the J. C. Quagga Company here. What
about the Arsenal now, eh?' I took some notes.

'Ah, they're a good team, Mr R.,' Robinson went on, 'but they'll
never beat the Arsenal. Wait till they come down to London, they'll
be slaughtered.'

The conversation continued for five minutes in similar vein, and
then Mr Robinson said, 'By the way, I've just had some more of
those Naples plum peeled in. You know, you had some a few months

ago. Yes, tasty, eh? Twenty? Right, I'll send them off today. Thanks very much.'

'You see?' Mr Robinson said. 'It's easy. Now you try.'

I looked in the address book and selected a firm in Manchester. Nervously I asked for the number and was put through to a Mr Elliott.

'Hello, Mr Elliott?' I said brightly. 'It's old Bennett of the J. C. Quagga Company here. What about the Arsenal now, eh, Mr Elliott?'

'I am not a footballing man, Mr Old-Bennett,' Mr Elliott said sharply, 'but I am glad you telephoned. Is Mr Robinson there?'

'Not at the moment,' I said, 'but he asked me to send you his regards.'

'When you see him,' Mr Elliott said, 'ask him if he would consider taking back those Naples tomatoes he sold me last month. I can't shift them.'

'I'll tell him', I said.

I looked at Robinson and shook my head sadly.

'Not to worry', Robinson said. 'Now listen to Mr Fieldman. He has a different approach which may help you.'

Fieldman was a young man, and a snappy dresser. He looked altogether too prosperous, and I had not taken to him. He had two telephone techniques; either he put on his public school voice and talked about rugger and the stock market, or he told nasty jokes in a leering drawl. He was particularly successful, I was told, with pineapple chunks. I listened to his call to the manager of a small supermarket chain in the Midlands.

'Mr Kennedy, old boy?', he said, 'CF of JCQ here. Lovely day, what? Business thriving? Marvellous, wonderful!'

I thought to myself, 'I could never do that, not for all the pineapple chunks in Queensland.'

'I was having a few jars at the club on Saturday after the game,' Fieldman continued, his voice getting oilier, 'and I heard a lovely story and thought "I must remember that for old Kennedy." It appears that this girl. . . .' He then proceeded to tell a joke so monstrous in its distortion of the female anatomy, and so wildly optimistic in its description of masculine performance, that if Mr Kennedy had been a person of even moderate refinement he would have replaced his receiver and gone away to be quietly sick in a corner. In fact I heard him laughing all the way from Coventry, and Fieldman then proceeded to sell him a huge load of Naples plum peeled tomatoes, and twenty cases of pineapple chunks.

Fieldman sat back, smirking. 'That's how to do it, old boy', he said.

I tried again, this time it was Mr Fitt of Newcastle. I did quite well. I said, 'What about the Arsenal, eh?' and Mr Fitt said, 'What

30

about the Magpies then?' I was about to change my approach in mid-stream and tell him about a blue tit I knew, thinking that he was a bird watcher, but just in time I realised that "The Magpies" was the nickname of Newcastle United. Mr Fitt talked at great length, under the impression that I was a true enthusiast, and finally said in a very friendly manner, 'Nice to talk to you. Give me a ring any time', and rang off.

'Well?' said Robinson, 'What did he say?'

'He said that all the Magpies need is a good centre half and a reliable goalie and they would romp the championship', I said.

'What about tomatoes?' Robinson said.

I blushed. 'I forgot to ask him', I said.

With Mr Applestone of Bristol I tried the hard sell. I tried persuasion and flattery, I urged, and finally begged him to try our tomatoes, with a small measure of success.

'Well', said Robinson, whom I was beginning to hate. 'What did he say?'

Trying to keep pride out of my voice I said, 'He will try them.'

'Good lad', Robinson said with such genuine pleasure that I began to like him again. 'What will he take?'

'He wants a tin, to sample', I said.

'One tin? One bloody tin? We can't send him one tin. You mean one case. No one orders one tin. He must be mad.'

'Well he wants one tin. It's my first order, and I'm going to send him one tin.' I glared at him. 'From little oaks, tiny acorns grow', I shouted, beside myself with fury at the insult to my first customer.

Emboldened by my success, I telephoned Mr Shimmer in Plymouth. 'Mr Shimmer', I said, forgetting about the Arsenal, 'I've got some beautiful Naples plum peeled tomatoes, just arrived from, er, Naples.' I told him the price and the size of the cans. 'How many can I send you, Mr Shimmer?' I asked briskly.

Mr Shimmer was delighted. 'Just what I need', he said. 'The last shipment I had from you went very well. How many can I have?'

Just then Mr Quagga walked into the office. 'Scrub the tomatoes, boys', he said. 'Tomkins has taken the lot.'

'You can't have any, Mr Shimmer', I said. 'Hard luck', and I slammed down the phone and went out to lunch.

Economic Batch Re-ordering Quantities Related Importwise.
Management by Objectives

I was alone with Mr Quagga in his office. He said, 'Well, you have been with us two weeks, and you must have gained some useful knowledge. What have you actually sold?'

'One hundred cases of pineapple rings, fifty of skinless ham, and one tin of tomatoes', I said modestly. My big sale, a large one by our standards, had established my reputation. It had not been difficult. One day whilst the others had been at lunch a telephone call had come from a major wholesaler, who barked, 'Quagga? Send me a hundred cases of pineapple rings and fifty skinless ham. OK?' Before I had time to praise the Arsenal he was gone.

'I knew that you could do it', Mr Quagga smiled. 'Now I want to discuss the expansion programme that I have in mind. It is dairy produce.' He waited for my reaction, which was to stifle a yawn, but when I saw that he was disappointed, I gripped the arms of my chair, half rose from my seat, opened my eyes wide, and fell back, overcome. This seemed to satisfy him.

'Our new department will be entirely in your hands. You will purchase, and you will sell. According to your reference, you are an expert on cheese, but I have heard of a new product which sounds interesting. It is margarine with ten per cent added butter. Find out all about it, keep me informed of your progress, and remember that I am here to help you. Good luck!' He stood up and clasped my hands with both of his for so long that I was suddenly worried.

'You may rely on me, sir', I said, looking him straight in the eyes and resisting an overpowering urge to salute.

'Good man', he whispered huskily.

Critical Path Analysis as Applied to the Importation of Highly Non-Durables

There is a technique in Management Consultancy which goes under the awe-inspiring name of 'critical path analysis'. It has always been a favourite of mine, combining roundness of phrase with utter incomprehensibility to the layman. Its superficial sense of desperate urgency has clients reaching for the cheque books in mild panic, and it was a clever man who invented it.

The critical path method is a technique for planning a project by breaking the entire operation down into its component parts, and then rearranging them into the exact logical sequence in which they must be performed. Each operation is timed and costed in order that the programme can be brought to a satisfactory conclusion at the right time and at the right price. One can produce an entire wall-covering of graphs and diagrams, using a multitude of coloured inks, and charge a substantial fee.

Of course, another name for critical path analysis is 'getting organised', but this is an altogether less expensive phrase which is not recognised by Management Consultants.

Unfortunately I did not learn about critical path analysis until many years later, a pity, because I could have done with some of it in the J. C. Quagga Dairy Produce Division.

I started correctly enough. From the commercial attachés of the French, Dutch and Danish embassies I obtained details of produce available for export, and I selected a Dutch company which specialised in margarine with 10 per cent added butter. A telephone call to their Rotterdam office soon had me in possession of price, quantities, and delivery.

I ordered five tons, packaged in half pounds, and then I telephoned all our customers and proceeded to sell this exciting new product at a price which I had carefully worked out to be competitive, yet give us a nice profit. Within three days I had sold the lot, and I took my colleagues to lunch as a celebration, talking airily of what we could do to Unilever.

At the time I had a girl friend called Susie, and I thought that it would do me no harm at all to call my new product after her. Mr Quagga suggested a name incorporating freshness, like Spring Meadow, or Summer County, but I assured him that such a name had no chance, and anyway Susie was very fresh. All my customers seemed satisfied with it, and Susie herself was delighted.

My five tons finally arrived at Hull docks, and I wrote out dozens of despatch instructions to the wharf and sat back, waiting for repeat orders. A beautiful operation, completed with the minimum of fuss and maximum efficiency, in the true tradition of the City of London merchants.

An unexpected telephone call from Hull interrupted the speech I was drafting for the Lord Mayor's banquet. Could they please have details of my import licence. What import licence, I said. Ha ha, they said, my licence to import five tons of margarine with 10 per cent added butter. They could not touch my Susie without it.

I rushed to the Ministry of Food, but it was Friday afternoon and there was no one to help me. I spent a miserable weekend, with visions of five tons of margarine melting and slowly engulfing the city of Hull.

The Kindly Face of Bureaucracy

On Monday morning I poured out my troubles to a ministry official and received a stern reprimand, but eventually I was given my licence and my margarine was free.

Then things began to go wrong. An irate manager of a northern Co-op called me. 'I can't sell your margarine', he said. 'I've just had a ministry inspector here and he has made me withdraw it.'

c

'What's wrong with it?' I asked, bewildered.

'He tells me', the manager said, with a certain disbelief in his voice, 'that the printing is wrong. Susie is too big.'

'They haven't', I said, shocked to the core, 'printed a pornographic drawing of Susie on the packet, have they?'

'No,' said the manager, suddenly interested, 'but if you have anything like that, I could sell it up here.'

I slumped in my chair, waiting. Sure enough the ministry inspector was on the phone within five minutes. He explained nastily that I had committed a serious offence. Apparently it was not permitted to have the brand name larger than the word 'margarine', and 'Susie' was too large. He gave me the regulation number, the paragraph number and the sub-section number of the law that I had broken, and in a daze I made a note of them on the paper that contained my speech for the Lord Mayor's banquet. I was instructed to inform all my customers that Susie must be withdrawn from sale.

Once again I rushed to the ministry, and after a mere five hours I found the official who dealt with illegal printing on margarine packets. It was a lady, who listened to me with cold eyes and clenched lips.

'Before I make a decision in this case,' she said, 'kindly show me your authority to use the name Susie on your product.'

'I have no authority', I said. 'I did not know that I had to have permission. I am very sorry.'

Having got me on the run, the lady was not going to let me off easily.

'We, at the Ministry of Food, are meticulous in the extreme when it comes to giving brand names to foodstuffs. We will not allow the public to be misled, and we frown upon frivolous and suggestive names. Even if you had submitted Susie as the name for your product, we should have rejected it out of hand.'

'If you knew Susie, like I know Susie . . .' I sang, hoping that a little joke would ease the situation, but I could see that my case was hopeless.

'What must I do?' I said.

'Either withdraw the product for repackaging, or sell it for canteen catering purposes where its illegal name and printing will not be exposed to the general public. Meanwhile we shall consider whether prosecution will be necessary.'

Back at the office I telephoned all my customers with the sad news, and they were furious. Then I knocked at Mr Quagga's door, and was greeted politely but coldly. I told him the story and he listened in silence.

'It could have been worse', I said. 'No one wanted to return it.'

34

'Do you know why?' Mr Quagga said. 'Because they bought it very cheaply. Cheaper, in fact, than we bought it.' He smiled icily. 'Kindly inform me how your price was established.'

'Simple', I said. 'I just divided the price of a ton by the number of pounds in a ton, and added our profit.'

'Do you have your calculations available?' Mr Quagga said.

'Of course', I said, producing my note book. 'Here you are. One ton, divided by 4,220 . . . oh.'

'Exactly', said Mr Quagga. 'How many pounds are in a ton?'

'2,240', I said.

'And what is 4,220?'

I pondered. 'The length of the Nile?' I suggested.

'Possibly', Mr Quagga admitted. 'Or perhaps the height of Ben Nevis?'

'I think it's a bit higher than that', I said.

'Well,' said Mr Quagga, 'the interesting, if unorthodox method of dividing a ton by the length of the River Nile has led the company into a substantial loss. Tell me, do you think you are suited to commerce? Why not try for a position in the civil service?'

I stood up, and we shook hands. As I left, he said, 'Preferably the Egyptian civil service.'

Chapter 5

Job Description Anomalies. Benevolence of Domestic Credit-Finance Companies

Being without employment twice in a season is a bad start to any businessman's career, but it did not shake my determination to reach the top. I had not yet found my niche, I assured myself. Studying the classified advertisements, I found several jobs available under the heading of 'Collector-Salesman'. I did not know what a collector-salesman was, but it had an attractive ring to it. I had always been a collector, of stamps, coins, matchbox covers, and even golf balls. The golf ball era was in my very early days, and I used to sleep with my collection under my pillow. I offer no explanation for this bizarre hobby, but I loved my golf balls, and used to polish them and even talk to them, although I cannot recall any actual conversations. I would strongly deny any Freudian solution, and unfortunately it did not indicate any incipient golfing talent, although I do believe that I am the only man in golfing history who lost three balls with his first three shots at the first hole.

As for the 'salesman' part, had I not already proved my ability by selling a tin of Naples plum peeled tomatoes, which I had never seen, to a man whom I had also never seen? A collector-salesman's job was made for me, and I decided that it consisted of selling stamps to philatelists, first editions to bibliophiles perhaps—a nice refined esoteric occupation calling for the strictly amateur qualifications that I could muster.

I telephoned the advertiser who had placed the most grammatical advertisement, and spoke to a Mr Hymish.

'Any experience?' he asked.

'I have collected stamps,' I said, 'golf balls. . . .'

'Comedians,' said Mr Hymish, 'we don't want.'

I went to see Mr Hymish, who must have been desperate for staff, and I was rather depressed by the appearance of his establishment, which was in a non-glamour area of London. I was also depressed by the appearance of Mr Hymish. Sallow, thin, with receding black hair and a Charlie Chaplin moustache, he did not inspire confidence, but he was good-natured enough, and quite pleasant to his newest recruit as he explained what a collector-salesman does.

A collector-salesman, or tallyman, as he is known colloquially, sells merchandise, usually clothing or household articles, on credit to the general public in their own homes. He is not a door-to-door salesman who calls once and is never seen again, but he builds up his own round of customers and calls upon them weekly, collecting their instalments and selling them more goods on credit, gradually building up their debt to the company and keeping it at a high level. He is not, it was explained, a shark battening on the poor, but a benefactor, supplying shoes for the children, blankets for the household, and labour-saving devices for the housewife that, but for him, they would have to do without. Care was always taken that no one's debt ever became too burdensome, and since the tallyman called regularly, he developed a friendly relationship with his customers, knowing their requirements before they did and knowing exactly how much they could afford to pay.

Thus did Mr Hymish convince me where my future lay. Basically I always wanted to be a philanthropist, and here was my chance to go amongst the poor distributing warm clothing. I would have liked to distribute hot nourishing broth also, but my recent clash with the food industry had persuaded me to keep well clear of that business until we had both recovered.

I accepted the job that Mr Hymish offered me, and I knew instinctively that I was going to be one of the world's great collector-salesmen. This would be my way to the stars.

Non-Control of Stock Controllers. Footwear Marketing Differential

I started my new job next morning and met my fellow collector-salesmen. They were a disreputable looking bunch, slightly raffish, and definitely easy-going. Most of them had circles under their eyes, like seedy playboys. Upon their arrival they deposited with the upstairs office the money they had collected the day before, and picked up their Wednesday books. Then they went to the stores and selected the items they had to deliver to their Wednesday customers. I watched them. Alf was first.

'My King's Cross day today', he confided. 'Very rough lot.'

He checked his list and began to call out his requirements to the storeman, who was a miserable old goat, like most of his ilk.

'Pair of men's shoes, black, size eight', Alf demanded.

'Out of stock', the old storeman said happily.

'Give me brown then', Alf said.

'Out of stock', the storeman said, beaming.

'Give me size nine then', Alf said. 'Old man Dunlop won't notice. It's his half-day and he'll be drunk.' He crossed the shoes off his list. 'One underset, black, WX', he said.

'Only pink left', the storeman chuckled.

'That'll do. So long as I put it on her she won't mind the colour.' He winked at me.

'What is an underset?' I asked.

'Slip and knickers', Alf said. 'Two double blankets, blue, and two pairs of sheets.'

'Only white blankets left', the storeman said joyfully.

'Gor blimey George,' Alf said, 'you're having a field day today. Give me white. Got any of those Belgian rugs left?'

With obvious reluctance the old man admitted that there was plenty of stock.

'Give me three brown ones then', Alf said.

'No brown left,' George crowed, 'blue and red only.'

'I'll take the red', Alf said.

I went with Alf to help him load up his van, and asked him if he anticipated any trouble with his customers, since very few of them would receive the goods they had requested.

'No,' said Alf, 'they won't mind. So long as they get something. They seem to think that they're getting it for nothing, anyway. Most of them have been paying me their few bob for so long it's become a habit, like the rent, and they take what I give them. I've got them well trained', he grinned.

When all the salesmen had been dealt with, Mr Hymish said to me, 'Right, we are now going out on your round. I shall be coming with you for the first week to introduce you to your customers and show you how to sell.' We filled his car with a vast assortment of clothing and set out for Cricklewood, in north-west London, for my initiation.

Our first call was upon Mr O'Reilly, a grey-haired gentleman of the labouring classes. Mr Hymish collected his fifteen shillings, marked it down in his book, and introduced me to Mr O'Reilly, who shook my hand civilly. His concrete-lined palm removed several layers of skin from my knuckle. Mr O'Reilly had obviously had something on his mind. He moved awkwardly from one foot to the other, and finally said to Mr Hymish, 'Them boots you brought me last week. . . .'

'A lovely pair of boots', Mr Hymish said. 'What a lovely pair of boots I brought him last week', Mr Hymish said to me.

Mr O'Reilly, a slow speaker, started again.

'Them boots you brought me last week, they hurt my feet.'

'They hurt your feet?' Mr Hymish said in a low voice, disbelief in each syllable.

'They hurt my feet, sorr', said Mr O'Reilly. 'They are not at all comfortable, sorr.'

Mr Hymish held his moustache between finger and thumb, adopt-

38

ing a thinking position. Then he spoke in measured tones, like a Queen's Councillor.

'Tell me, Mr O'Reilly, were they not—working boots?'

'Yes sorr', said Mr O'Reilly, 'They was working boots.'

Mr Hymish took a step backwards, opened his arms in a gesture of appeal, and addressed me.

'Working boots he expects to be comfortable', he said. 'Not enough that they were the best leather money can buy, waterproof, soles an inch thick, lovely quality laces, he expects working boots to be comfortable already.'

I was obviously supposed to make some response, so I gave a short nervous laugh. Mr Hymish turned back to Mr O'Reilly.

'What were you going to do with these working boots, eh? Go to a dance? Have a . . . a hooley, whatever it's called?'

Mr O'Reilly began to see the error of his ways. He grinned embarrassedly, but Mr Hymish continued his attack.

'Working boots', he said, beginning to laugh, 'not comfortable, he says.'

Mr O'Reilly began to laugh. I began to laugh. Within seconds we were all rocking with merriment. Mr O'Reilly pulled out a red handkerchief and mopped his eyes, and Mr Hymish stamped his little feet uncontrollably.

'But . . .', said Mr Hymish, so suddenly and sharply that we all stopped laughing, 'if you want a nice comfortable pair of boots, a pair of boots like velvet on the feet . . .', he lifted his eyes to the sky and clasped his hands together, 'then next week I will bring you such a pair of boots like you never wore before. All night you can dance at the Shamrock Club.'

'I'm sorry, sorr, about the working boots', Mr O'Reilly said. 'I wasn't t'inking at all, them being working boots, I mean. But you can bring me a nice comfortable pair next week, sorr.'

Mr Hymish's expression became stern. 'On one condition', he said. 'Will you promise me something? These new boots you will not use for working. Only pleasure boots. OK?'

Mr O'Reilly accepted this condition.

'Five shillings deposit, please', said Mr Hymish whipping out his pen and making an entry in his book in one smooth movement. 'A pleasure to do business with a gentleman', he added as we left.

We continued our round, collecting and selling, for the rest of the day. Almost all our customers were women, and at most of the houses we were welcomed like friends of the family. Mr Hymish was liked and respected by everyone, to my surprise, and the fact that he was the manager calling on them personally, put them on their best behaviour. Uncountable cups of tea were offered to us and accepted, and it soon became apparent that one of the chief requirements for a successful tallyman was a strong bladder.

Between calls, Mr Hymish regaled me with stories of his early struggles and triumphs, liberally sprinkling them with helpful hints.

'Once,' he said, 'when I was broke, I took a job as an icecream seller at a cinema. One afternoon the manager sent me up to the balcony, but there was only one person there so I came down again. The manager was furious. "I thought I sent you upstairs?" he said. "There's only one woman upstairs," I said, "and she bought a choc-ice." The manager said, "And who are you to decide that she mustn't buy another one?" And he sent me back again.'

We sat in silence while I digested this story.

'Did she buy another one?' I asked.

'No', he said.

I puzzled long over this tale, and at the end of the day I really felt that I had learned something valuable, but I could not think what it was.

The Implacement Theory Related to the Mirrored Image Society

On Friday morning Mr Hymish said, 'Today we are going to start you off on a brand new round.'

'How do you start a new round?' I asked him.

'This particular one was started by the photographer canvassers', he said. 'We find a new housing estate, lots of young couples, and therefore lots of children. A photographer canvasses every house, offering to take photographs of the children. He chooses the right time, when the kids are back from school and the husband isn't home from work yet. No mum can resist having pictures taken of her kids. When the photos are printed we frame them and take them back to the mothers. That is what we are going to do today.'

We loaded his car with two large boxes and set off for a district near London Airport. During the journey I took the opportunity to look at the photographs. They were all enlarged to eight inches by ten inches, in poor quality colour, and the frames were a crude study in thick plywood and mirrored glass.

At the first house was Mrs Gimp. 'We have a surprise for you', simpered Mr Hymish, and produced from behind his back a yellow and pink apparition with crooked teeth. Mrs Gimp melted and gurgled. 'Beautiful', she breathed.

'Just what we thought', said Mr Hymish. 'My wife, she loved the little darling so much she wanted to keep it herself.'

Mrs Gimp snatched the photograph. 'How much is it?' she asked.

'Three pounds nineteen and six', said Mr Hymish.

'But I haven't got it on me', said a disconsolate Mrs Gimp.

'We don't want it, madam,' said Mr Hymish, 'at least not all at once. You can pay for it over twenty weeks, no interest charges, just four shillings weekly. Mr Bennett here will call on you until you have completed payments.'

Mrs Gimp was very satisfied with these arrangements, and I made out a little payment booklet for her. She gave me four shillings, and a sixpence for myself. It was the first time anyone had ever given me a tip, and I was thrilled. 'Do I have to declare it for income tax?' I asked Mr Hymish. 'No, son,' he said, 'I'll save you the trouble. I'll deduct it from your wages.'

Mrs Harris two doors away was a different case. Both her children were on the photograph, the boy standing stiffly behind his sister with his hand on her shoulder as though having just delivered her a sharp blow.

'I don't know,' Mrs Harris said doubtfully, 'I don't know at all. It's not a very good picture, and it's a lot of money. Also, it's blurred. They must have moved when he took it. It's a lovely frame, though.'

Mr Hymish said, 'The frame alone cost three pounds ten. We don't make any profit out of this, you know. We do it because we love kiddies, and we are trying new photographic experiments. Look at the movement in this picture. You can see the little loves moving, can't you?' He gently swayed, moving the photograph to and fro.

'That's what I don't like', said the harassed Mrs Harris. 'They are always moving, my kids, never still for a moment. I'd rather have a still picture.'

Mr Hymish tried another approach. 'But I haven't told you the most important thing yet, have I? This picture has been selected by Metro Goldwyn for their "Beautiful Children" competition. With your permission, of course, they may be required to come to the Savoy Hotel for the final. If they win, it means a contract. Would you be able to take a couple of weeks off to go to Hollywood, Mrs Harris? All expenses paid, naturally. Not your husband, just you and the kids.'

Mrs Harris pondered. 'I wouldn't mind a few days away, particularly without the old man. It would serve him right', she said, showing the first signs of enthusiasm. 'He can get his own bloody meals for a change.'

'Four shillings please', said Mr Hymish, and another client was on the books.

Poor Mrs Wilson gave us the hardest time. Even Mr Hymish did not have the bare-faced effrontery to suggest that the Wilson offspring had an outsider's chance with Metro Goldwyn. She was badly cross-eyed, with but two teeth like fangs. Little Miss Wilson was going through a bad period. She could have been cast as Dracula's daughter without using a scrap of make-up.

Mrs Wilson said, 'My husband would kill me if I spent four pounds without asking him first.' I sympathised privately. I would have killed any wife of mine who spent four pounds on a photograph of Miss Wilson.

Mr Hymish shrugged. 'Too bad', he said. 'Mr Bennett, remember to take the little girl to the crusher tomorrow.'

'Right!' I said, and I made a note in my book, reading out the words as I wrote: 'Mrs Wilson's little girl to the crusher tomorrow.' I had no idea what I was talking about.

'What's the crusher?' asked an apprehensive Mrs Wilson.

'Well, you see, madam, any photograph of an unwanted child must be destroyed', said Mr Hymish. 'It's to do with copyright. We have to be very careful about unwanted children. We have a special machine, government inspected, a huge machine with three big spikes.' He extended three fingers. 'One spike goes here', digging one finger in the picture's right eye, 'one spike goes here', sticking the second finger in the left eye, 'and the third here', putting his thumb in the mouth, 'and suddenly—twist, scrunch, rip, tearrr', at the same time twisting his hand violently. 'The photograph must be utterly destroyed without trace. Poor little unwanted girl', he said, brushing away a tear. I had a lump in my throat.

'Give it to me', said Mrs Wilson, pulling the photograph from his hands.

'Four shillings, please, Mrs Wilson', said Mr Hymish.

'Take some photographs and do the next street by yourself', said Mr Hymish. 'I'll meet you in the café in an hour.'

It was sheer bad luck that my first knock at a door was answered by a man. He was in shirt sleeves, and looked grumpy.

'I have brought the photograph of your two little boys', I said. I offered him the picture of two young bruisers.

'Photograph?' he said. 'I didn't order any photograph.'

I had a hard time with Mr Wilkes. When I told him the price I thought he was going to hit me.

'Three pounds nineteen and six for a picture of them cheeky little buggers!' he exploded. 'You've got to be joking, mate.'

I tried the 'Beautiful Children' competition, and he nearly choked himself laughing.

'Right,' I said, 'it will have to be the crusher then.'

'What's the crusher?' he said.

I explained, with full actions and utter realism. If Metro Goldwyn had seen me, they would have given ME the contract.

Mr Wilkes had a gleam in his eyes. 'Show me again,' he said, 'the scrunching bit.' I showed him, almost breaking a finger in my enthusiasm.

"'ere,' said Mr Wilkes, 'wait there a minute.' He disappeared into his house, and returned a few moments later with an armful of photographs. 'Can you do these for me?' he said. 'This one is me wedding photo. Try and get the spikes here and here, me wife's mother and brother, the lazy sod, and this one. . . .'

'Sorry, Mr Wilkes,' I said, 'our crusher only does children.'

Going home in the car, with a mere three photographs unsold, Mr Hymish said, 'You've got a good round there. Thirty-three customers, each paying four shillings a week. You will collect for three or four weeks, finding out who are the good payers, and then gradually you will introduce them to our other merchandise. If it's a cold day, you tell them that we supply electric heaters or fur lined boots. If it's wet, raincoats and wellingtons for the kids. Slowly you build them up. Next week you will collect six pounds twelve shillings. Within six months you will be bringing in fifty pounds a week from this lot. You'll make a lot of money, my boy, at one and six in the pound commission.'

'It will be a pleasant change', I said. 'But what about the women who want to know when they have to take their children to the Savoy for the finals of the beauty contest?'

'Think of the money you're earning,' said Mr Hymish, 'and the answers will come to you in a flash.'

The Skilled Tradesman. A Proud Tradition in Job Enrichment

One morning all the salesmen were summoned to a meeting, where we were given a pep talk by Mr Hymish about a great new addition to our service. This was 'made-to-measure' suits for men. We had always tended to concentrate on our women customers, throwing the males of the household the occasional pair of shoes. A tailor from head office was present, and he gave us detailed instructions on how to take measurements. It was made as easy as possible for us. Forms were provided with full details of the essential measurements that were required, and all we had to do was fill in the form accurately. Back neck to waist, shoulder to elbow, all the way down to the wrist, inside leg and turn-up width. It was easy. Instant tailoring. With some ceremony we were each presented with a tape-measure and a book of suitings.

Special rates of commission were promised, and a contest was arranged with an un-named prize of immense value for the man who sold the most suits in the first month.

I decided that I was going to win this contest, as I had already won the quilt-and-pillowcase and the green underset contests.

I prepared for the made-to-measure like a true professional. I made a list of all the men on my rounds, and planned my calls so that they would be at home when I arrived. I had one superb suit, a fine grey flannel creation, and I removed the Kilgour, French label and neatly replaced it with my own company's less distinguished name. Then, with tape measure at the ready, I set out to win.

From the start my campaign was a success. Without exception my customers took one look at me and said, 'You look smart today', or 'Look what the cat's dragged in.' Almost invariably, with that wit for which Londoner's are renowned, I was asked if I was going, or had just been, to a funeral. With no difficulty I was then able to raise the subject of our wonderful new hand-made suits, and although the men in general showed little enthusiasm, their womenfolk insisted that they wanted their men also to look as if they were dressed for a funeral.

The measurements were easy to take, except for one: the inside leg measurement. This was, for me, sheer purgatory. Surrounded as I was by the family, with the husband standing sheepishly in front of me, I had to slip my hand between his thighs. 'Open your legs', I would hiss, and my customer would shuffle his feet another inch apart. 'Pull your trousers up', I would whisper angrily, and then, with infinite care I measured the distance from his crotch to his shoe. I tried several alternative methods of taking this hated measurement. I tried guessing, and even taking the measurement on the outside of the leg and gauging where the point of the crotch should be. The experience, however, did seem to establish a certain rapport between my customer and myself, and thereafter we were exceedingly polite to each other.

I romped away with the made-to-measure contest, selling eighteen suits to my nearest opponent's five, and Mr Hymish was delighted with me.

'At this rate', he said, 'you'll be a supervisor in no time, and in a couple of years I wouldn't be surprised if you became a manager. I knew you had it in you, as soon as I saw you.'

'What is my prize?' I asked him, putting first things first.

'A made-to-measure suit', he said.

'I've got a suit', I said. 'Can I have the money?'

The great day arrived when the suits were delivered, and I took Mr Sid Ackerman's to him straight away. I had always thought that there was far too much mystique attached to the art of tailoring, and it pleased me that I was as good as any Savile Row man after a mere ten minutes instruction.

Mr Ackerman, a mild man, was pleased to see me. His wife was a thin, acid-tongued creature, the type that often marry these gentle ones. She insisted that her husband tried his suit on there and then, and I sat full of confidence, waiting for him to emerge from the bedroom in all his glory. The glory, as he stepped hesitantly into the living-room, was only marred by his crotch, which was hanging between his knees.

'It's a nice suit', he said kindly. 'The trousers only want taking up a bit perhaps.'

Mrs Ackerman wailed, 'What have you done to him?'

I sat like a stone, feeling my face go white.

'You've ruined him', Mrs Ackerman said, unfairly I thought. 'He looks like a duck.'

'Not a duck, Mrs Ackerman, surely', I said, trying as always to be accurate. To me he looked more like a penguin.

'A duck!' she insisted. 'He looks crippled. My poor Sid.'

'The jacket is a lovely fit', Mr Ackerman said bravely.

'Yes,' I agreed, 'the jacket is perfect. Just walk up and down, Mr Ackerman.'

With difficulty, Mr Ackerman complied.

'You've made him so short', Mrs Ackerman complained. 'I've never seen Sid so short.'

'Try walking with your legs together', I advised Mr Ackerman, in the absence of any more positive ideas.

'What are you insinuating', Mrs Ackerman roared. 'My Sid always walks with his legs together. He's known for it', she added.

I took out my tape measure, more as a weapon of defence against Mrs Ackerman than for any remedial reason. 'Pull your trousers up, Mr Ackerman', I said. He obeyed my modest request, and sure enough the crotch fitted perfectly. Unfortunately the waist-band then reached his chest and the legs ended halfway up his shins. Mrs Ackerman left the room, and her husband and I eyed each other moodily. 'You've done it this time, son', Mr Ackerman said. 'It's not me, you know that, but the old girl's properly upset. There'll be trouble', he added, unnecessarily.

Mrs Ackerman reappeared with two of her neighbours. Clad in overalls, they came in and stood with arms folded solidly, uttering wordless sounds of distress and revenge.

'Well?' said Mrs Ackerman.

'I was in the tailoring', one of the neighbours said. 'It's the inside leg, it's six inches too short.'

'Fancy doing that to your Sid', said the other. 'And he's always had a high crotch, I've remarked about it.'

'Take that suit off at once, Sid,' ordered Mrs Ackerman, 'and you

45

can just give me my deposit back and take the suit away with you.'

'With pleasure, Mrs Ackerman', I said, pulling out my wallet. I had got off lightly. I thought I was going to be lynched.

I threw the suit in the back of my van and drove away, a very worried tallyman. It was a fair assumption that if Sid Ackerman's trousers were wrong, the other seventeen made-to-measure trousers were also wrong. I tried to think of a way out, but barring the unlikely event that overnight the men's fashion world would announce that low crotches were in, there was none. I said nothing to Mr Hymish when I returned to headquarters, and the deposit that I returned to the Ackermans I paid out of my own pocket.

In the morning, I collected all the remaining suits and delivered them, knowing that the men would be at work. This was only putting off the day of retribution, but a man has only so much courage, and another seventeen episodes like that with Mrs Ackerman were not to be endured.

It was on Saturday morning, the only time when my men customers were able to come to the warehouse, that the affair reached its inevitable conclusion. I arrived late, and I heard an uproar from the direction of Mr Hymish's office. A voice was saying, 'I'll kill the bleeder when I see him', and another voice, easily identifiable as Mr Hymish's, saying, 'No, Mrs Watson, excuse me, but I'll kill him myself, give me that privilege.' I collected my Saturday book and tip-toed out of the front door, but I saw three couples coming towards me carrying boxes so I went out the back way and began my Saturday round.

I returned late to the warehouse, hoping that no one would be there, but Mr Hymish was sitting in the dark showroom, legs crossed, staring at a rail which had a long row of men's suits hanging on it.

'What did I ever do to you', he said when he saw me, 'that you should do this to me?'

'Nothing. . . .' I began.

'Wasn't I a good boss to you? Didn't I look after you like my own son-in-law?'

'Sure. . . .' I said.

'Now, all of a sudden, you deal me a killer like this. Seventeen suits, made-to-measure, all with little short legs. . . .'

'Eighteen', I said, pleased to get in a constructive word. 'Here is Mr Ackerman's suit that I had in the van.'

'Eighteen', he repeated. 'It used to be my lucky number.'

In the gloom, we sat in silence, looking at the rail.

'This job is not big enough for you', Mr Hymish said at last. 'You want to go somewhere you could do really big damage. You know where you want to go? The War Office.'

'Thank you for your suggestion', I said. 'And you? What will you do about the suits?'

'Me?' he said. 'I'll sit here and wait, please God, for a Drury Lane production of Snow White and the Eighteen Dwarfs.'

Chapter 6

The Production Executive and the Grass Roots Background Tradition

Having learned all that there was to know about selling direct to the public, it was time for me to take my next step up the ladder towards my eventual target of Business Supremo. My knowledge of catering, food importation, weekly credit-and-selling techniques, and bespoke tailoring, would stand me in good stead in the future. Now was the time to enter the field of production.

The absorbing mysteries of the factory floor had to be explored. The very words 'shop floor' filled me with an emotion which I found hard to explain. Perhaps it was fear of the unknown, of the rough, salt-of-the-earth folk upon whom our economy is based, or perhaps it was extreme boredom.

Yes, for me it was the shop floor, production, strikes, sit-ins and walk-outs, the noble art of making things instead of flogging them, and having set my sights upon this worthwhile objective, I eventually reached it through sheer determination.

This is not true.

What actually happened is that I met a little, round, fat man at a party, who claimed to have known my grandmother. Mr Gownstein was a dress manufacturer, and after questioning me at length about my career he said, 'You must come and work for me. I need a production manager.'

I protested that I knew little about dresses and nothing about production, and I had never, in fact, set foot in a factory.

'You went to college, didn't you?' Mr Gownstein asked with some impatience.

'Yes,' I said, 'but I studied geography.'

'Geography shmeography', said Mr Gownstein. 'So all right, I got a factory in Aldgate and another one in Peckham, and one up in Scotland somewhere, so there's your geography already.'

Faced with this unanswerable logic, with one bound I became a production manager.

Method Study in Factory Procedure. Value Decision. Control Theory

Mr Gownstein and I had a talk in his office on the Monday morning that I started work in his factory. He had a flattering faith in my ability.

48

'All you have to do', he explained, 'is feed work into our three factories and our outdoor workers, order fabrics and trimmings, supervise the pattern cutters, do all the new costings, keep accurate records of our production on a day-to-day basis, liaise closely with the sales and despatch departments, and make sure that no one spends too long in the toilets. All right? You'll soon pick it up. Anything you want to know?'

'Yes', I said. 'This is so vital and skilled a job, with so much depending on it, and there are probably so many excellent production men available, that I should like to know why you chose me.'

'A fair question', Mr Gownstein said. 'You are young, and I know you must be clever because I knew your grandmother, and what a clever woman she was, and I need someone I can trust, and I just have a feeling that you are going to be OK, and also you were cheaper than a proper man.'

'There is a well-known saying', I said, 'that if you pay peanuts you get monkeys.'

'In this business', he grunted, 'we are all monkeys, otherwise we would be dentists or solicitors.' He lit a very large cigar, and looked at me solemnly. 'All we get in this lousy business is aggravation', he said.

We then made a tour of the factory, and I met the heads of each department. 'This is our new production manager', they were told. 'Be careful, he is going to be tough.' Then the tough new production manager was shown to his office in a corner of the cutting room where he huddled in his chair, terrified to emerge in case someone asked him something.

A knock at my door produced severe symptoms of fear. I was sure that I was going to be asked to negotiate a price with a pattern cutting outdoor worker who had just spent two hours in the lavatory, but it was kindly, motherly Edie, the machine-room manageress who looked as scared of me as I was of her. 'Ooh, sir', she said, in a voice so weighty with anxiety that panic overwhelmed me, 'Sir, do you want tea or coffee?'

I waited a moment, to let my blood turn back to blood again, and then I made my first decision, firmly, without a tremor.

'Coffee please, Edie', I said.

'Made with water, or all lovely milk?'

'With all lovely milk', I said, gaining confidence every second.

'How many sugars?'

'Three!' I barked, and Edie scuttled out. I would show these workers who was boss. There was nothing to this production business.

Edie returned, wearing her perpetual worried look.

D

'We've run out of coffee,' she said, 'so I brought you tea.' So I learned my first lesson in production management, which is 'Always Expect Things to Go Wrong'.

My second experience was far more traumatic. One of the girls in the cutting-room knocked at my door and asked me to put the radio on, and since this was possibly the only thing in the entire factory that I could do with some degree of confidence, I agreed. I switched on, but a very aggrieved girl returned a few moments later. 'You've put on classical music', she said, outraged. I listened. A man was singing 'Roses of Picardy'. 'That's not classical', I said. 'It's "Roses of Picardy".' 'I don't know what you call it,' she said, 'but me and Dor call it classical.' Her expression made it clear that from now on, in her estimation, I was One of Them. I retuned the radio to something indisputably non-classical, and immediately my buzzer buzzed. It was Mr Gownstein screaming, 'Turn that bloody wireless off.' I pressed wildly at another button, and switched on the fire alarm.

In a weird detachment I saw my entire work-force troop out of the factory. They walked calmly and quietly, with no trace of panic, and I watched them go with a certain pride. Mr Gownstein came rushing up the stairs into the cutting-room, closely followed by two of the packing department staff. Their arms were loaded with net dresses.

'Where's the fire, where's the fire?' Mr Gownstein shouted. 'Get the old evening dresses from under the cutting-tables.'

'There is no fire, Mr Gownstein', I said. 'It was a mistake.'

'No fire?' Mr Gownstein said, stricken. He dropped the dresses in a heap at his feet. 'Put them back, boys', he said sadly. Then he rushed out into the street, shouting, 'Everybody back, false alarm, everybody back.'

Mr Gownstein explained to me that I had lost ten minutes production time for a hundred and twenty people, and that was a total of twenty hours, which was an inauspicious start for a production manager on his first morning. 'If you make these mistakes,' he advised me, 'at least make them during lunch time.'

The Decision Theory in Practical Application

I returned to my office to hide, but I was not left in peace for long, for Edie came to see me carrying a piece of material over her arm. I managed to disguise my trembling by tapping on the desk with my fingers, and I looked at her with a special look which I invented on the spot, combining the impatience of a busy man who did not want to be disturbed with the kindliness and knowledge of a benevolent oracle.

'What is it now, Edie?' I asked.

'It's this, sir', she said. 'Should it be run and turned out or bagged out?'

I studied the piece of material closely, playing for time, and rubbed it thoughtfully between my fingers. I deduced quite quickly that it was probably cotton, and possibly part of a dress, so I nodded as though I realised the deep significance of her question. Run and turned out, or bagged out. If only I knew what she was talking about. Obviously Edie, an experienced woman, was undecided as to the two methods, and therefore, my logical mind assured me, either one could be used.

I made up my mind. If I was to endure this torture daily without exposing my total ignorance, I would have to make decisions and stick to them through thick and thin.

But which one? Run and turned out sounded like someone being forcibly ejected from a pub, whereas bagged out gave the impression of someone in the last stages of fatigue through constant association with loose women. Attractive though the latter was, there was a certain dactyl splendour in the other phrase which appealed to me.

'Run and turn it out, Edie', I said, and she went happily back to the machine-room.

This particular decision theory, a technique well known to Management Consultants for helping to make decisions under conditions of uncertainty and risk, has since become known as the 'run and turnout/bag out (or ratbag) theory', and it carried me through many a tight corner in my career as a production manager. In brief, when a decision is required and the experts are undecided, then in nine cases out of ten either will do, and the time saved in debate more than compensates for the rare error.

The ratbag technique did not, of course, carry me through all my problems. The manageress of the cutting-room, a capable, shrewd woman called Katie, saw through my act within two minutes of our first conversation. I think it happened when she indicated 'that nice pink lay' on the far cutting-table, and I suddenly went all hot and blushed to my fingertips, and Katie explained that a 'lay' is the term for layers of fabric stretched on the cutting-table, sometimes as high as twelve inches, prior to being cut. I thought she was pointing at her youngest cutting assistant, Doreen.

'You haven't been in this business long, have you?' Katie said.

'No,' I admitted, 'not long. Since nine o'clock, actually.'

'You'll need help', Katie said. 'Come and see me if there is anything you want to know. I'll keep the secret.'

The Essence of Firm Staff Control

If Katie was my support and guide, her two youngest cutters, Maureen and Doreen, known as Mor and Dor, were the bane of my life. They were barely competent girls of nineteen or twenty, with bad posture and flabby figures who always wore fur edged bedroom slippers, and they slopped around the room like two large, soft question marks. They had no interest in their work, and were only content when the radio was pouring out pop music, to which they wiggled and sang. Woe betide any disc jockey who dared to play anything remotely approaching a ballad. On one request programme, an old lady asked for 'Bless This House', and the indignation of Mor and Dor was so vividly expressed that I threatened to turn the radio off permanently.

'It's all right for you', Mor said. 'You like classical music, don't you. You like "Rosie from Piccadilly" don't you?'

' "Roses of Picardy" ', I corrected her, allowing myself to be drawn into a discussion which I could not possibly win.

Vera, the intellectual of the cutting-room, sprang to my defence. ' "Roses of Picardy" is a beautiful song', she said. I could have done without Vera's help.

'It's all right for you old ones', Mor said, turning Vera purple with fury. 'You don't know what music is, do you? Violins and harps is what you like, ain't it?'

'Why,' said Vera, 'you cheeky little bitch. . . .'

'Don't you talk to me like that', threatened Mor. 'I'll smash your face in. . . .'

Vera and Mor advanced towards one another. Dor was shouting, 'Do 'er, Mor', and I was shouting, 'Please, ladies. . . .' and then Mr Gownstein walked in.

'Quiet!' he bawled. 'Get back to your work', and then he said to me, 'What's all this about?'

'Well,' I said, 'it all started when Gracie Fields sang, "Bless This House". . . .'

'All right', said Mr Gownstein. 'That's enough to upset anyone.'

Selection of Upper Echelon Managerial Material

At the end of my first year, Mr Gownstein made me a director of the company, but any idle thoughts that I might have had about buying a bowler hat and an umbrella, and joining the Institute of Directors, were quickly dispelled. I was summoned to his office, where he told me the good news and handed me a very small glass of whisky.

'I've only given you a little drink, because I don't want you snoring this afternoon', he said, pouring himself a triple.

52

I thanked him for the confidence he had in me.

'It doesn't mean anything', he said.

'Oh?' I said.

'No more money.'

'Perish the thought', I told him. 'Can I have my name on the door?'

'Why?' he asked. 'Everyone knows who you are.'

'My name on the company paper?'

'In about two years, when we've used up the old stock.'

'You do not anticipate', I asked him, 'that it will change my life in any way?'

'Oh yes', he said. 'You will have to work harder.'

I gave him back the whisky. 'I don't think that I'm ready for the honour', I said. He poured my whisky into his own glass.

'There's director's fees', he said.

'How much?'

'Not much', he said. 'We are losing money. It's been a lousy season.'

'Any other advantages?' I asked.

He pondered for a while. 'You can attend board meetings', he said, 'if you are not busy.'

This was it! At last I would have the opportunity to make my mark in British Industry, to attend Top Level Conferences and make Vital Decisions Affecting the Lives of the Workers. I would be hard, shrewd and incorruptible, but still retain that twinkle in the eye that would betray my humanity and paternal affection for the labouring classes from whom, through sheer thrust and ability, I had sprung.

Let me raise the lid from the mysteries of the board-room, to prove that those who have the power also have the frightening responsibility to keep the future secure for their employees. Take, for example, the meeting of senior management at the Gownstein Dress Manufacturing Company Ltd.

Present: the managing director, Mr Hugh Gownstein.
  the assistant managing director, Mr Willie Gownstein.
  the sales director, Mr Arthur Camphorn.
  Me.

The meeting opened with a statement by the managing director, short and tubby, with grey curly hair. Mr Gownstein, a self-made man if there ever was one, presided in his large swivel chair. This was a massive creation, remarkable for the carved wooden balls which decorated its arms and back. Mr Gownstein always wore cream silk shirts and a monocle on a black cord. Unfortunately, he could never keep the monocle in his eye, and in times of stress, when it tended to whirl around his body, he would impatiently hang it over his ear.

The gist of Mr Gownstein's address was that we were about to commence the manufacture of a budget range of dresses—budget means cheap—to be marketed through a new company.

Mr Willy, Mr Gownstein's son, a tall thin man with a long pointed nose, thoughtfully scratched his nostril with a tyre pressure gauge. Mr Camphorn, a bloodless man with straw coloured hair and a Mongolian slant to his eyes, nodded wisely. He often nodded wisely, but rarely did anything else. He was a man who knew his limitations.

I yawned. You see, we had known all about the budget range for three months.

'What we want to do', said Mr Gownstein, 'is think up a name for the new company, something snappy, sexy, catchy but dignified.'

I sat up. This was a chance to participate in true decision making in the best tradition of board-room meetings. I narrowed my eyes.

'Don't go to sleep, Gordon', bawled Mr Gownstein. 'I'm talking to you.'

'I was merely narrowing my eyes', I protested.

'My eyes haven't been too good lately', said Mr Camphorn. 'I keep getting the twitch.'

'You want to stop bloody nodding all the time', said Mr Gownstein. 'You give me the twitch every time I look at you.'

Mr Willy Gownstein said we all gave him the twitch, and why did we not continue with our meeting instead of shouting at each other. We agreed. Mr Gownstein jammed in his monocle, which immediately fell out again, Mr Camphorn nodded wisely, and I leaned forward alertly, like they do on television.

'What do you think of "Frances Farmer"?' said Mr Gownstein.

'Why "Frances Farmer"?' said Willy. 'I don't like it. "Farmer" sounds like a country bumpkin. We want a sophisticated image, something like, for instance, "Polly Piccadilly".'

'What!' yelled Mr Gownstein. 'Sounds like a cheap West End tart. You'll be saying "Lily Leicester Square" next.' He laughed immoderately and alone.

Arthur Camphorn coughed apologetically. 'How about "Prudence Pricket"?' he said.

' "Prudence Pricket" ', said Willie disbelievingly. ' "Prudence Pricket"? Where did you dream up that stumer?'

Arthur twitched. 'I've always liked the name', he said. 'It's my wife's cousin's name. Lovely girl, fair, about twenty-nine, a good stock size 14.' Two small red spots appeared high up on his white cheeks. Aye aye, I thought.

It was time I took a hand. 'If you want a name combining

sophistication, elegance, charm and wealth, I suggest "Beverley Belgravia".'

'Too long', Willie said. 'Too much of a mouthful. We want something short and sweet, like "Susan Small". Can't use that, of course, we're thirty years too late.'

Mr Gownstein's little eyes gleamed mischievously. ' "Lucy Large!" ' he shouted. We all laughed.

'Or better still', he went on, flushed, ' "Bertha Bigti . . . tch tch tch . . ." ' His secretary had just walked in.

'I don't know why you bother, Mr Gownstein, I'm sure', she said, as she put four cups of Nescafé on the table. 'You know I can hear every word you say through these thin walls.'

'We weren't saying anything rude, Mavis, by my life we weren't', Mr Gownstein swore away his fifth life that day.

'You'll get a pimple on your tongue, you will', said Mavis as she flounced out.

'On my tongue I can stand it', Mr Gownstein grunted.

We started again. The suggestion 'Linda Leisure' was followed by 'Denise Dewdrop', 'Mabel Maytime', 'Christine Court', 'Sally Slimtrim'. Mr Gownstein was getting bored.

' "Fanny Fanackerpan" ', he chortled.

' "Lousy Liza" ', countered Willie. We roared.

' "Lottie Longdrawers" ', screamed Mr Gownstein, hammering his fist on the table in merriment.

Willie lay back in his chair, braying helplessly. Arthur was sitting upright, hooting and twitching desperately. Names were flung furiously about the board-room, no one listening to anyone else's suggestion. Mr Gownstein, completely overcome by his last obscene if colourful contribution, slowly slid off his chair and lay on the floor, heaving.

Arthur squeezed out, ' "Droopy Deidre" '. Willie wheezed ' "Nittie Nettie" '. His tears had started the lengthy journey down his nose.

I looked at Mr Gownstein. His face was blue, he was choking.

'Willie!' I shouted. 'Help him. His monocle's caught in his balls.' It was one of the momentous sentences of my life. Mr Gownstein's monocle was stuck between the carved balls on his chair, and the cord was strangling him.

Willie coughed out, ' "Bessie Bumface" ', and curled up. Arthur was holding his heart and spasmodically jerking. I rushed to Mr Gownstein, but I could neither release the cord nor lift him. Luckily I had some nail clippers attached to my key ring, and I cut the cord.

I knelt down by Mr Gownstein. He was breathing very heavily, and muttering through pale lips. Some last message, perhaps, a final

55

instruction about the bust dart on style 4372. I put my ear to his mouth.

' "Nancy . . . Knickerleg . . ." ', he gasped.

Gradually the commotion ceased. Mr Gownstein, fully recovered, sat scowling at his son, who was wiping his eyes, letting out an occasional sob. Arthur Camphorn sat inscrutable as ever.

The meeting quickly ended. The new company was given the name 'Frances Farmer' and went into voluntary liquidation within six months.

Personal Relationships in Business. Ergonomics in Direct Manufacturing Techniques

Friendship is perhaps the noblest human relationship. It builds character, it brings joy and comfort, it relieves loneliness and depression; it can be the basis of a fuller and happier life, and it can produce examples of self-sacrifice which shine like beacons in our dark, wicked world.

So much for philosophy. This being a strictly practical business manual, it must be firmly stated that friendship is not a basis for a business relationship. There are exceptions to this rule, naturally. If you are broke, for instance, and you have a very rich friend who says, 'Let us go into business together, old pal. Do not worry about money, for I have enough for both of us', then go ahead, and I wish I had your luck, but in fact the situation is hypothetical because rich men do not have poor friends.

Even when partnership is not involved, a business connection between friends should be avoided, because if things go wrong one stands to lose a friend as well as money. In the rag trade, where friendship is at a premium, this warning is doubly justified.

Consider the affair of Jack and me. Although we were scarcely in the inseparable category, I had known Jack for many years, and had sympathised with his strenuous efforts to become a tycoon. His progress had been minimal, not necessarily through lack of ability, although undoubtedly his career had been hampered by a genuine reluctance to get out of bed before half past ten. Yet he was often to be seen at two in the morning in the Bayswater Road, full of enthusiasm for whatever task he had set himself, so no one could accuse him of laziness.

Jack was a buyer and seller of anything mechanical. Cars, cash registers, combine harvesters were all grist to his mill. He bought them, repaired them and sold them, sometimes at a profit. Despite the fact that he was always trying to unload something on to me, I had been successful in retaining our friendship while continually rejecting his bargains. They were not difficult to reject. 'Jack,' I recall saying to him, 'what would I DO with a chicken plucking machine?'

Our business paths collided when he called on me, with some excitement, to say that he had become the owner of a small dress-making workshop, and could I supply him with work. Apparently he had visited this factory to buy some ancient overlock machines from the Greek proprietor, and after some hours of negotiation, had purchased the entire establishment, including staff. The Greek gentleman had found it desirable to leave the district permanently, and had accepted from Jack £100, a 1952 Buick, an obsolete fire-engine with bell, and a potato peeling machine, with which he intended to set up in business somewhere on the west coast of Scotland.

'You are crazy, Jack', I told him. 'There is no tougher business than being an outworker in this trade.'

'Don't kid me, boy', Jack said. 'I happen to know that there are fortunes being made by making-up units like this.' He then proceeded to give me a list of people he knew who started from nothing and bought their first Rolls Royce after six months.

It should be explained that garment manufacturers, owing to chronic staff shortages in the industry, often have to make use of independent contractors known as 'outdoor makers', or simply 'outworkers'. An outworker's unit in the dress trade is usually a small concern, very often run by a husband and wife team with a handful of machinists, and it is a precarious way of making a living. In a good season money can be made, but should the spring be wet, or the summer cold, or the winter mild, or should the newest fashion prove unpopular, then the outworker is the first to go to the wall. On the other hand, if he is a skilful cutter, and can make a garment from a smaller quantity of fabric than the manufacturer has allocated, then the surplus material, known as 'cabbage', is the outworker's jam on his bread and butter. Outworkers have grown rich on cabbage, but experience and knowledge are essential.

'No one makes fortunes from my company, Jack', I told him. 'We don't pay enough. Also, you won't make any cabbage from me, I'm too careful.'

I could not dampen his enthusiasm, so I agreed to visit his factory to see if his staff were capable of making my dresses. Perhaps they were, but since they only spoke Greek I was unable to be sure. Certainly they were the most villainous looking women I had ever seen outside the chorus of 'The Beggars' Opera', but I watched them machine some blouses and they appeared reasonably competent, so, being desperate for extra production, I sent him 250 dresses that demanded the simplest technical knowhow. Jack, rapidly picking up the essence of the business, promised me prompt delivery and a high standard of work, and then complained that he was losing money on the deal.

I telephoned Jack at approximately ten-minute intervals for progress reports. In between my calls to him, he called me, and we worked each other up into a state of extreme nervous tension.

'How's it going, Jack?' I asked for the tenth time that day.

'Lovely, boy', Jack said. 'I'm short of zips, though.'

'Impossible', I told him. 'I counted them out myself.'

'Are you calling me a liar?' he asked threateningly.

'Yes', I said.

There was silence while we both seethed, and simultaneously hung up on each other. Then the phone rang two minutes later.

'I found the zips,' Jack said, 'but the pattern must be wrong. My girls can't get the sleeves in.'

Summoning all my technical knowledge, I advised him, 'Keep trying.'

'Yeh, OK', Jack said. 'I'll go and shout at them a bit.' Then he phoned back. 'They've all walked out on me,' he said, 'so I'm going to the pictures. I'll speak to you tomorrow.'

To my surprise and relief, he delivered the order on time. The standard was not good, and there were twenty dresses short, but I had had far worse results from more experienced outworkers in the past.

Jack worked hard in the next few weeks. He taught himself to operate all his machines, and to repair them. I gave him all the help I could, and allowed him to spend hours watching my own cutters operate, and at the end of six weeks he was convinced that he knew everything. It was the height of the season, and he had been able to obtain well-paid work from other manufacturers to keep his little workshop in full production. He even learned some Greek swear-words which enabled him to communicate with his staff, and I was so impressed with his progress that when he asked me to supply him with a new contract I agreed, and sent him five hundred pinafore dresses, simple sleeveless garments buttoned down the front.

'You'll be careful with them, Jack?' I said, anxiously. 'It is an important order. Are you sure you can manage the cutting yourself?'

'Don't you trust me, boy?' he said. 'Haven't we known each other for ten years? Have I ever let you down?'

'All right already with the rhetoric', I said, lapsing into the vernacular. 'Just be careful.'

It was on the third day that Jack phoned me. 'You don't happen to know the Greek for "Get on with it, you stupid cows", do you?' he asked, in a voice trembling with emotion.

'Try kindness, Jack', I urged him. 'Smile at them, use charm. Get them to fall in love with you.'

He phoned back in half an hour. 'They've all walked out on me again', he said.

'What about my dresses?' I asked flatly, reaching for a tranquilliser.

'Nothing to worry about boy. Half of them are made, just waiting for buttonholing. The other size is all laid up on the table, and I'll cut it tonight.'

'I'm coming round to see you, Jack', I said. 'I want to be sure they are all right.'

As I entered Jack's factory I heard the whirr and thump of his buttonhole machine. Jack was sitting there, all alone, buttonholing dresses with every appearance of expertise. Before I could say a word he stood up and said, 'I told you not to worry. I can operate this buttonholer better than anyone.' He picked up a dress from the heap and offered it to me. 'What about that?' he said with pride. 'Isn't that a great buttonhole?'

I examined it. 'It's a good buttonhole, Jack', I said. 'Not a great buttonhole, but a good buttonhole.'

'And the colour?' he said. 'Is that a good match?'

'El Greco himself', I told him, 'could not have done better on the colour.'

He sat down, smiling with huge satisfaction, and prepared to continue his work.

'Don't do any more, Jack', I said.

'But they're nearly finished', he protested. 'Why stop me when there's only half a dozen left?'

I held the dress up. 'Because you have buttonholed them round the hem', I said.

He scrabbled frantically amongst the dresses, picking them up, looking at them, and discarding them.

'Christ', he said. 'What a waste of buttonholes.'

We looked at each other in silence. 'What can we do?' he said finally.

'A suicide pact?' I suggested.

'Can't you sort of incorporate the buttonholes in the design?' he said. 'Maybe buttonholes around the hem will catch on. You can hang little gold charms from them. . . .' He saw my face, and stopped.

'I shall endeavour to explain your ideas to Mr Gownstein in the morning,' I said, 'just before apoplexy sets in.'

'How about cutting the hem off?' he said. 'They will come up a bit short, that's all.'

'Six inches short', I said. 'Would you cut six inches off the bottom of your trousers?'

'Well,' he said, 'it's no use crying over spilt milk. I've got another lay to cut tonight. Half your order will be all right.'

He walked to the cutting-table, piled nine inches high with layers of shiny poplin, and started the cutting knife. I was surprised to find him both accurate and fast, until he came to a difficult part, right in the centre, which he could not reach. To my astonishment, instead of walking to the other side of the table, he climbed on it and knelt on the lay.

'Jack,' I said in alarm, 'be careful. You'll ruin it.'

'You worry too much', he said. 'I always cut this way. It's quicker.'

The table creaked as his fifteen stone bulk crawled along the surface, and then, with a splintering sound, the table collapsed. I watched Jack slowly disappear, head first, into a hole until he was lost from sight. With soft swishes, layer after layer of poplin, pink, blue, turquoise and lemon, followed him. It was beautiful, like a Walt Disney interpretation of Birth, shown backwards. Deeply moved, I walked to my car, composing as I went my letter of resignation to Mr Gownstein.

Chapter 7

The Power and the Source. The Interfirm Comparison Technique for Potential Senior Management, and the Interview Co-Determination Method

Where lies the source of power in the land? In Parliament? The army? The trade unions? Who knows for certain where power lies in Britain. We only know one thing; we know where it does NOT lie, and fairly prominently in the list of places where it does not lie comes The Gownstein Dress Manufacturing Co. Ltd. I therefore had no regrets about leaving, and I decided that my best chance of achieving personal power was to join one of the nation's immense commercial empires, like ICI or Courtaulds, and work my way to the top. I was aware that it would take me forty years, and there would be stern competition, but someone had to be chairman, and there was no point in aiming at the target anywhere but the bull's-eye.

I wrote letters of application to the Top Twenty in the Big Business League, and settled down to wait the rush.

Some of my letters were unsuccessful. Nineteen in fact. But the formidable and mammoth Galactic and World Distributors, as they were modestly called, affectionately known in the City as GAWD's own company, invited me to meet the managing director of the manufacturing division. This was indeed a breakthrough. GAWD had 100,000 employees, and a multitude of interests covering every possible legal method of extracting money from anyone who had something to spend.

My interview with Mr McTavish took place in the GAWD building, a solid but austere edifice that would undoubtedly have been requisitioned for the Gestapo HQ had London been occupied in 1940. I quickly realised that GAWD did not throw their substantial assets around on unnecessary luxuries, and I made a mental note that when I became chairman I would have the curtains washed.

Mr McTavish was a small peppery Scotsman. How often small men control our destinies, I thought. Perhaps that was my trouble, I was too big. However, I felt myself shrinking during my interrogation.

'So,' Mr McTavish said, glancing at my letter on his desk, 'you are a production manager. What technical qualifications do you hold?'

'None,' I said, after some thought, 'not actual technical.'

'What qualifications of a non-technical nature?'

'None,' I explained, 'not actual qualifications.'

'I see', he mused. 'Can you make a garment throughout?'

'Certainly not', I said.

'Make a pattern?'

'No.'

'Cut?'

'No.'

'I see', he repeated, clearly at a loss. He studied my letter of application again, looking puzzled. 'You mention here', he said, 'something about photography . . . men's bespoke tailoring, ah, yes, margarine, and here . . .', he turned the page of my letter, 'tomatoes . . . ach, never mind. Just tell me what you actually did as a production manager.'

My mind went blank. Nearly three years of my life suddenly vanished. What HAD I done at Gownstein's? All I could think of was controlling the radio, and slamming my door to shut out the sound of Mor asking Dor whose side Australia was on in the war.

'Mr McTavish,' I said, 'I produced five thousand dresses every single week of the year, except Christmas week. I did not design them, nor cut them, nor machine them, neither did I pack and despatch them. I just produced them.'

'No doubt', sneered Mr McTavish, 'through prestidigitation.'

'Not at all', I said, wondering if Mr Gownstein would give me my job back. 'Through organisation, administration, hard work, and the ability to control my staff.'

'We do not employ people like you', he said, 'as production managers.'

'The loss is yours', I told him as I stood up to leave.

'But we can always use good administrators', he continued, waving me back to my chair. 'One of my companies needs a sales controller. Are you interested?'

'Which company?' I asked.

'The Titania Brassière Company.'

'I know nothing about brassières', I said doubtfully.

'Neither do I,' said Mr McTavish, 'and I am chairman of the company.'

'I can start on Monday', I said.

The Executive-Operator Relationship and Control Technique

Everyone knew Titania Brassières. Everyone, that is, who travelled on London's tube trains, because their advertisements were everywhere. They were not sexy advertisements, like the ones for Silhouette and

Superform, the ones responsible for the swift intake of breath through the teeth. Titania had workmanlike advertisements, remarkable for the accurate blueprint-like quality of their illustrations, with little arrows directing the attention to points of interest such as the 'floating self-aligning cups', and the 'supa-soft, satin-sprung stretch-straps'. No glamorous girl walking through the palm trees in her bra from Titania, but a nice respectable young lady, smiling and oozing kindliness, wearing two solid hemispherical dartboards on her chest, as firmly secured as a parachute harness.

Titania's offices were in the centre of London's West End, and I was met in reception by the sales director, who was my immediate superior. He was a friendly man, a neat, clean American named Godfrey Barron, who told me, with no hint of embarrassment, to call him God.

God explained that my job was to help him control the activities of the numerous salesmen that Titania employed. There were fifty of them, covering the British Isles very thoroughly, with eight divisional managers, two regional sales managers, and a national sales manager, all apparently watching each other.

'What shall I do first, God?' I asked him.

'Write to each of the managers, introducing yourself', God suggested, so I drafted a memo very carefully. I was anxious to make a good impression, and I aimed at a friendly dignity, thoroughly British, indicating that although I was new I would brook no nonsense, and I endeavoured to hint, between the lines, that they would be dealing with someone destined to become one of the great sales controllers of the brassière world. This called for a literary talent beyond my abilities, but I finally satisfied myself with this:

'Dear . . .
I would like to take this opportunity to introduce myself. I am your new sales controller, and I intend to work closely with you in order to make your task as a sales manager with Titania Brassières Ltd as pleasant as possible. Your co-operation is requested, and I look forward to a long and mutually rewarding relationship.
Yours sincerely,
G. Bennett.

God's secretary typed all the memos and I signed them, feeling that I had done a good day's work. God picked up a memo, read it, and said, 'Jeeze, what's this?'

'My letter to the managers, introducing myself', I said.

'I'll show you how to do it', God said, and called his secretary. 'Take this, honey', he said and began dictating.

'Hi, John, I'm the new guy replacing Cyril, and I would sure like you to call me . . .' God turned to me and said, 'Gordon sounds a bit sort of stuffy. How about "Gordy"?'

'No,' I said, 'not "Gordy".'

'Don?' he suggested. 'Buddy?'

'Just Gordon, please', I said.

God shrugged. 'OK, Gordon then. I would sure like you to call me Gordon', he continued. 'John, you and I have one helluva job to do, fella, if we aim to keep Titania at the top of the heap. Feel free to call me anytime, anywhere, John. If you need me in the evening or at the weekend, my home number is . . . what's your home number?' he demanded. Not being quick witted enough to say that I was not on the telephone, I told him, and down it went into the memo. 'I guess you and I are going to have a lot of fun together, John, beating some get-up-and-go into our salesmen. By the way, John, try to push style 17137 this week, will you? We're losing out on this great bra, John, and I know you will try to push it in wherever you can. Make this week a style 17137 week, John, and keep beating it into all your men. Get them to say "17137 is the nearest thing to heaven" every time they speak to you on the phone. John, we have a great future in a great company. It will be a real pleasure to meet you at the sales meeting on Saturday at the Greenland Hotel. Be there real early, John.'

God leaned back in his chair. 'That's the way to write to these deadbeats', he said. 'Never write to them without pushing them', he advised. 'Never praise them without criticising them; never criticise them without praising them. All the time, push, push, push. Gee, these guys have got to be pushed.'

'What's this about a sales meeting on Saturday?' I said.

'The southern divisions are coming in on Saturday morning', he said. 'I'd like you to be there early, OK? I'm introducing a new bra, a beautiful black version of our famous Equalabra. You know the Equalabra?'

'Not offhand', I said.

'A truly great bra', he said. 'Padded, circlo-stitched, comfortised cups. You must know it.' He seemed genuinely distressed.

'Yes, God, I'm sure I must have run into it somewhere or other', I said, soothing him. 'A great bra.'

Product Knowledge: the Essence of Successful Marketing in Single Sex Commodities

Brassières, an item of clothing that had never loomed large in my life, began to dominate it. I was astonished at the never-ending variety. There is absolutely no equivalent to the brassière in any

64

garment worn by a man. A sock, for example, is a sock. It can be long or short within reason, natural or man-made fibre, plain or patterned, but there the possibilities end. Men do not wear socks to the thigh, or barely covering the toes. They do not wear socks of a transparent material through which the ankle can be clearly observed. They cannot buy a sock, for instance, with a false heel, so that the foot appears larger than it really is. There are no attachments on socks which can be cunningly adjusted to make the instep fuller, or to force the toes apart. Socks do no come in thirty basic sizes, and there is only one way to put on a sock; the most ingenious designer has failed to find an alternative, such as over the head.

Brassières stand out in the field of human clothing, as unique garments.

Product Appreciation and Incentive Inventiveness at the Intro-Plan Level

Mr Godfrey Barron was the only truly single-minded man I have ever known. He was totally dedicated to the selling of brassières. He loved a good salesman like a son, and his contempt for a bad sales-man was akin to hatred, and was terrible to witness.

On the morning of the sales meeting he called for me at an impossibly early hour, and before I had shut the car door he was telling me about his incentive plan to encourage the sales of the new bra, the Black Equalabra.

'What do you think of gold stars?' he asked.

'Very nice', I said, not having the faintest idea what he was talking about.

'Each day a man sells ten dozen or more, we will send him a gold star. How do you think that will go down?'

'A nice gesture', I said.

'And a silver star if he sells six dozen,' he said, becoming enthusi-astic as the idea took shape, 'and a red star if he sells three dozen, and a green star if he sells two dozen.'

'How about a black star if he sells nothing', I suggested as a little joke, but God jumped upon the suggestion as though it held the touch of genius.

'Gee, Gordon, what a great idea. A black star cancels out a gold star.'

I asked the question that had been bothering me, half expecting a rude answer. 'What will they do with the stars, God?'

'We'll run an eight-week contest, and the one with the greatest number of gold stars wins the prize. The Gold Star Contest, we'll call it. Fantastic!'

E

'What will they do with their other coloured stars?' I asked.

'At the end of each week they can change their coloured stars for gold ones. Two silvers for a gold, three reds for a silver, three greens for a red.'

'It will take some organising, God', I said.

'Never mind', God said. 'You can do it.'

'What will the stars be made of, God?' I asked.

'Yeah,' he said, 'that is the problem. We'll give it some thought. We can't cut them out of coloured foil, because I know these guys, they'll all suddenly be in the tin foil star business, making their own like crazy.'

There was the sound of the urgent hooting of car horns.

'Jeeze,' said God, 'what's with these guys?'

'Well, you've stopped, God', I said. He had been so wrapped up in his scheme that the car had gradually slowed until it came to a gentle halt in the middle of the road. I had not liked to mention it, because I still held him in some awe. He accelerated away. 'Hell,' he said, 'I'm always doing that.' I made a mental note.

At the Greenland Hotel, Fred Carter, our advertising manager, and I arranged the tables to God's liking, and we three sat on a raised platform facing our audience. I sat in the middle, and I could see the salesmen looking at me, wondering who I was. God soon told them.

'This guy', he said, putting his hand on my shoulder, 'is the greatest sales controller in the business. What he doesn't know about bras and salesmen is not worth knowing. All right then, fellas, what about a hand for Gordon here!'

To my extreme embarrassment, I received a round of applause. It was given with stony faces, but it lasted a full five seconds.

God commenced the sales meeting. He was a good talker, but a long one, and for two hours he discussed selling techniques and past results, until everyone was beaten into submission. My admiration for him grew, but it was not shared by Fred Carter, whose vicious asides and mutterings of 'Sit down, you long-winded git' and similar witticisms helped to keep me awake.

After our coffee break, God stood and looked at his salesmen. He seemed to be casting a hypnotic spell over everyone.

'What is it', he began quietly, 'that you fellas have been waiting for?' No one told him.

'What is it', he continued, a slight thrill in his voice, 'that everyone has been asking for?'

'What is it', he said, raising his hands slowly, 'that your customers have begged you to give them?' He fell silent, and his eyes glowed. Despite myself, prickles ran up and down my spine, and a great excitement began to glow in my breast.

66

'What is it', God shouted, his arms high, 'that will make the women of this country say with one voice . . . GOD . . . BLESS . . . THE . . . TITANIA . . . BRASSIÈRE . . . COMPANY . . . LTD . . .?'

Exultation showed in the faces of the younger salesmen, and a kind of wonder. . . .

'Gentlemen,' God said, his voice now cracked with emotion, as a tear trickled down his cheek, 'let me present . . . Equalabra . . . in . . . BLAAACK!' Finished, he took a step back, his head drooped, one hand clutched his heart. . . .

Commotion overtook the room. Several men stood up and clapped, one actually climbed on a chair and shouted 'Three cheers for Mr Barron', but his manager could distinctly be heard snapping, 'Sit down you daft bugger.'

Fred Carter, in a pre-arranged ploy, suddenly flung open the door of an ante-room, saying loudly, 'And 'ere it is, blokes.' All eyes turned to the door. Nothing happened. Fred looked into the ante-room. 'Where's the silly moo gorn?' he said angrily. 'Oy, Cecilia!'

There was the sound of a toilet flushing, and a moment later a girl appeared at the door, wearing a long waist slip and a black bra, smiling brilliantly. Briskly she walked and turned, walked and turned, modelling her Black Equalabra. The salesmen followed her every move, some lecherously, some bashfully. The girl continued to smile, her eyes focused on no one.

God, recovered, was grinning at his audience. 'Isn't that something?' he said. 'What d'y'say fellas, isn't that something now?' A spontaneous cheer came from the men. At a flick of Fred's head, the model left the room. God sat down, saying to me, 'How did it go, Gordon?'

'Superb', I said. 'Absolutely super, God.'

'You think it went over well?'

'Marvellous', I said. 'Terrific.'

'You think they liked it?'

'They're crazy about it, God.'

He nodded. 'Wasn't too bad, was it?'

'Wonderful', I said, having to ration my superlatives, of which I was rapidly running out.

The Dramatic Interlude: an Instructive Technique Leading to Basic Knowledge Enrichment of Threshold Merchandise

'Now you've heard about it,' said God. 'now you've seen it, and now this is how you sell it in. You go to your buyer and you say, "Good morning, Mrs Buyer"—hey, Gordon, will you be Mrs Buyer?'

I stood up, feeling sheepish. Fred Carter, a stickler, obviously, for realism, picked up a square of white material from beneath a jug of water and tied it around my head, and wrapped the green baize table cloth around my waist.

He then attempted to roll up my trouser legs, but I kicked him sharply on the elbow. A storm of wolf whistles gave me a little confidence.

'Mrs Buyer,' said God, 'you are in business to make money. Am I correct?' He stood staring at me, six inches away, deadly serious, sincerity blazing in his eyes. Stage fright gripped me, and all I could do was grin at him.

'Are you interested in increased profit, Mrs Buyer?' he persisted.

'Yes', I squeaked.

'Suppose I told you that I can improve your turnover?'

I raised my eyebrows to their fullest extent, opened my eyes wide and shaped my mouth into an 'oooh'. As an impromptu piece of method acting it was not in the Marlon Brando class, yet it had a certain effectiveness.

'You have sold our famous white Equalabra for years, have you not?'

'Yes', I squeaked.

'And made a good profit on it?'

'Yes', I squeaked. I was not really satisfied with my dialogue. I felt that there was something missing.

'Well then, Mrs Buyer, I have some great news for you. I am so excited about it, I can scarcely contain myself!' To prove his point, he began to jig up and down. It was not fair, he had all the good lines. 'Mrs Buyer, in response to the request of thousands of buyers like you all over the country, we have produced Equalabra in BLACK'. The black brassière appeared in his hands like magic.

This was, I could sense, the dramatic high point of Act 1, and I put all I had into it. 'Great!' I said, with feeling. I threw my arms up in a gesture of exultation, and my skirt fell off.

It brought the house down.

'I cannot guarantee', said God, 'a similar reaction from all your buyers, but who knows?'

The Quantum Expense Evaluation Theory. The Tri-Stage Pitch Technique

Lunch time arrived, and I was left behind in the rush for the dining-room. I could see the salesmen jostling each other for seats, and although I was rather surprised at their behaviour, I thought, 'What a great tribute to our sales director, everyone striving to sit near him.' Not for the first time, I was mistaken; everyone was fighting to sit near Cecilia, the model, and God was all by himself. I took the seat next to him, and one of the divisional managers, a man with the appearance of a first-class crawler, joined us.

Before lunch was served, God said loudly, 'Remember, fellas, beer only, if you must have it. No one is permitted to order spirits or wine. If you want something other than beer, you must pay for it yourself. And go easy on the ordering; this isn't a party, it's a working lunch, and we must watch expenses. Remember, Mr McTavish checks the bills personally!' Having got this gracious speech off his chest, God settled down to enjoy his meal. He smiled at the DSM sitting on his left.

'Well, Paul,' he said, 'how are the children?'

I was astonished. God indulging in small talk!

'Very well, God, thank you', Paul said. 'The baby is getting . . .'

'You know, Paul,' God said, 'you can learn a lot from children.'

'You surely can', said Paul. 'Why, yesterday . . .'

'My own son, now', said God. 'You met him, Paul?'

'No', said Paul, disgruntled, realising that he was not going to be allowed to speak.

'My boy said to me last week, "Dad", he said, "bicycles are the greatest. All the boys at school have bicycles. Can I have a bicycle, Dad?" That's exactly how he said it.'

Paul and I looked at each other. Was this going to be a joke?

'Now,' God continued, 'I thought about my boy's words, and I realised something very significant. Do you see what it was?'

'Sure', said Paul. 'The kid wants a bike.'

'What my son had done', said God, ignoring Paul's over-simplification of the problem, 'was to make me a classic, natural sales pitch. First, he illustrates the desirability of the article. "Bicycles are the greatest." He tries to sell me on the joys of possessing a bicycle, see?'

We nodded, glumly. So much for God's small talk, I thought.

'Next,' says God, 'he shows me that everyone else has already discovered this desirable object, and that I had better get in on this great deal. "All the boys at school have them, Dad", he says. It's like you saying to Mrs Buyer, "So-and-so down the road has already bought Black Equalabra, and so have Jones Brothers at the other end of town. They're cleaning up.' You instil a little envy into the buyer, OK?'

'OK', said Paul, picking listlessly at his *hors d'oeuvres*, and no doubt cursing himself for sitting next to God. Burst of laughter were coming from the other tables, indicating joke time.

'Finally', said God, 'he asks for the order. "Can I have a bicycle, Dad?" he says. He carries his pitch through to the natural conclusion.

You can make the finest sales pitch of all time, but if, at the end, you haven't got the guts to come right out with, "Can I have your order please, Mrs Buyer?", then there will be no sale. Always ask for the order, Paul.'

Paul said he would, and he remarked how clever it was of God to analyse his boy's request so lucidly. I said to God, 'Did you buy your son a bicycle?'

'Hell, no', God said. 'What does he want a bicycle for?'

I was eating my modest steak, and God was toying with his boiled fish, when he suddenly choked. 'Jeeze,' he said, 'take a look at that, willya?'

We looked, but could see nothing unusual, except that Fred Carter had fashioned a brassière out of his paper napkin and was fitting it on his neighbour.

'What is it, God?' I said.

'That goddam Martin Rogers', he said. 'Asparagus, he's ordered. Have you seen the price of asparagus on the menu?' He was so aggravated he was near to tears. 'What a goddam pig. And Peters. And Johnson. All with asparagus.' He slammed down his fork in anger. I said a mental prayer that I, who had considered asparagus, had settled for mashed potatoes.

'And Fred Carter, he should know better, a senior company executive, what's he having?' The reason for his rage was the dish being prepared for Fred by his waiter, who was pouring liquids into a pan over a burner and igniting them.

'I think it's *steak Diane*', I said.

'Steak Diane!' said God, 'The son of a bitch.'

Paul had gone white. His waiter was now approaching, with all the paraphernalia—the trolley, the frying pan, the burner. He, too, I gathered, had ordered steak Diane.

'Actually, God,' I said, 'steak Diane is no more expensive than an ordinary steak.'

Paul flashed me a look of gratitude, but God was not placated.

'Fred is setting a bad example to the men', he said. 'It doesn't matter if it isn't expensive, it looks expensive, and if it looks expensive it shouldn't be ordered in front of the men. If he has asparagus too, I'll fire him, so help me. If McTavish was here, it would kill him.' The thought of the possible demise of our chairman temporarily put God in a better mood, but the sight of *crepes suzette* being prepared throughout the room, like warning beacons on the south coast during the Napoleonic wars, aroused him to fury again. He began a lecture on the necessity of keeping costs down in a commercial enterprise to such good effect that I rejected the cheese board out of hand, and Paul requested a glass of water instead of coffee.

70

The afternoon session of the sales meeting was entirely devoted to Black Equalabra, the selling of it, the advertising of it, the utterly irrestible qualities of every thread of it, and we had all had enough of it by five o'clock. God had a good idea. He suggested that I went out with one of the salesmen on Monday, to see at first hand how our new bra was received. Martin Rogers, the asparagus eater, was the salesman chosen, to his disgust. His area was Herts., Beds. and Bucks., and I arranged to meet him at nine o'clock on Monday morning outside his first call, a store in St Albans. I looked forward to watching a professional salesman at work, and I hoped that the little sketch in which I had participated would be of some help. I rehearsed Martin Rogers's opening speech: Good morning, Mrs Buyer. You are in business to make money. Am I correct?'

The buyer approached us. 'Hello, Mart', she said. 'You're early. What's up?'

'Had to be, Elsie', Rogers said. 'One of the head office men keeping an eye on me today.'

'Hope you don't want to sell me anything', she said. 'Your stuff's not moving out.'

'Give over', Rogers said. He pulled the new bra from his pocket and threw it on the counter, where it settled, quivering, like an octopus with two monstrous eyes.

'Equalabra', he said. 'Black.'

'Stick it!' said Mrs Buyer.

Statistical Analysis of Comprehensive Sales Records and Objective Attack Strategy

Wandering around the office one morning, wondering what I could do to reactivate the corsetry industry, it occurred to me that I had not yet filled in my football pools coupon. Always alert to the potentialities of a new system, I thoughtfully watched the girls in the sales department entering the latest figures on our card index. This was a highly comprehensive method of recording every transaction done with each of our thousands of customers. Information was copied from the salesmen's daily reports and invoices, and every customer's card carried details of the styles stocked, and the cash volume of business done. Each card was alphabetically filed within its town, which in turn was filed within its county. It was a superb system, expensively maintained by eight girls and a supervisor, and never, to my knowledge, used.

Today it was going to be used. I went into my office and sent my secretary to fetch the Yorkshire card index, while I studied my pools coupon. I started with my favourite club, Huddersfield Town. It was a matter of moments to calculate how much business Titania Brassières had done in Huddersfield in the past twelve months. It was £320. I was shocked! Only £320 for a town of 130,000 people! How on earth did Huddersfield hope to return to the first division with a paltry £320? Middlesbrough, a town only slightly larger, did £5,245. This indicated a certain win for Middlesbrough, unfortunately.

Liverpool, £9,936, and Manchester City £10,147, looked a fairly good draw.

It took me most of the day to find sixteen reasonable draws to put in my permutation, but I discovered some astounding figures. Reading, £3,985, was playing Crewe, £9! A home banker if there ever was one. I checked again, but there was no doubt about it. Nine pounds worth of Titania Brassières had been purchased in Crewe, a town of some 50,000 inhabitants. A quick calculation told me that there were probably 20,000 women of brassière-wearing age in Crewe, 19,990 of whom had never had the chance to wear Equalabra, black or white, to say nothing of Saucy Sweetness, Just Swell, or Mardi Bra. It did not bear thinking about! Poor Crewe. No wonder they were always languishing near the foot of Division IV. I called my secretary to take a letter to the manager of Crewe Alexandra FC. 'Dear Sir,' I dictated, 'I do not know whether you are aware. . . .' I stopped. I was being carried away.

Just then God came into my office for a chat. 'You've been busy today', he said. 'Anything interesting?'

'I have uncovered some useful information', I said modestly. 'Do you know, God, how much business we did in Huddersfield last year?'

'Tell me', God said.

'£320.'

'How big is Huddersfield?' God said. I told him.

That's terrible', he said, shaking his head in distress.

'But Middlesbrough,' I said, '£5,246!'

'No kidding', said God. 'A great little town, Middlesbrough.'

'You'll never guess what we did in Crewe', I said. '£9!'

'Jeeze,' God said, 'where is the goddam place? We must get some action in Crewe right now. Tell me more. This is great!'

By a happy chance the telephone rang, and I answered it. It was John Angel, our national sales manager, a superb salesman who carried most of our sales force on his shoulders.

'Is shag-face there?' John asked.

'By the sheerest good fortune, Mr Barron is right here, John', I said, and handed the phone to God.

'Hi, John', he said. 'How many dozens?' This was his standard greeting. 'Fifty-four and a half? Not bad, John. Where are you right now? Aberdeen? Gee, John, what are you doing up there? I need you down here, fast. You've only just arrived in Aberdeen? That's tough, John. See you in the morning, OK?' He put the phone down.

'Gordon,' he said, 'I think you have found us a new attack. I want the figures on every damn town and village in the UK.'

'God,' I said, 'it'll take weeks!'

'You can do it', he informed me.

I called my secretary. 'Get me the card index on Cheshire,' I sighed, 'and a lot of paper.'

John Angel arrived in the office next morning in a bad temper. 'What are you trying to do to me, God?' he said. 'Monday in Manchester, Tuesday in Newcastle, Wednesday in Aberdeen and Thursday in London. Are you trying to get me in the *Guinness Book of Records*?'

'John,' said God, ignoring his greeting, 'what do you intend to do with Crewe?'

John told us in a fairly uninhibited way what he would like to do with Crewe. God listened impassively. 'And what about Huddersberg?'

'Huddersfield', I corrected him. John had a succinct comment on Huddersfield.

'John,' said God, 'we have been guilty of a very serious oversight. Every week we check our figures—the amount of business done in each sales area. What we have NOT done up to now is to analyse each area, town by town. Now, I have some figures here that Gordon has prepared for us.'

John shot me a look of venom. I smiled at him.

'Area 61,' God read, 'covering Chesh-shire—£35,625 last year. Towns in order of size: Stockport £3,896; Birkenhead £3,423; Wallasey £1,986; Chester £3,045; Sale £2,443; Crewe £9.'

'Where did we go wrong, John?' God said, a deep sorrow in his voice. 'Why were we blind, John, to Crewe?'

'Most people are blind to Crewe', John snarled.

'And were we blind also to Huddlesford?' God said.

'Huddersfield', I murmured.

'The great city of Huddersfield,' God went on, 'Gordon tells me, is the home of the greatest football club in Britain.'

'Greatest what?' said John. 'Get out of it! Aston Villa is the best. . . .'

'Aston Villa', I corrected, 'has never won the First Division Championship three years in succession, like Huddersfield.'

'You know how many times Aston Villa has won the FA cup? shouted John. 'More times than. . . .'

73

'Fellas, fellas. . . .' soothed God. 'How much brassière business did we get out of Aston Villa last year, that's the question. Another question is, where the hell is Aston Villa, and who is the salesman?'

'Forget it, God', I said. 'Let's concentrate on Crewe.'

'Right!' said God, and he called Fred Carter, the advertising manager, into the office. 'Fellas,' said God, 'next week we start a blitz on Crewe. Fred, get me the prices for eight inch doubles and half pages in the local Crewe papers. John, arrange for the area salesman, the divisional sales manager and the regional sales manager to meet us at half past eight on Monday morning in a Crewe hotel. Gordon, get us all booked into the best hotel—well, not the best, but a clean one. And get out some more town figures for the area, and a list of every store and shop in Crewe that should be selling Titania brassières and isn't.' So, like an efficient military operation, the campaign was planned. John Angel was tight lipped about the whole affair. Fred Carter, on the other hand, was loose mouthed about it, particularly when he heard that he was included in the expedition to Crewe.

Promotional Field Marketing Procedure Adopting the Theorem of Anti-Variety Reduction in Miscellaneous Outlet Units

I can state categorically that there is a more depressing place on earth than the Vista Commercial Hotel, Crewe, at half past eight on a drizzling Monday morning. There is the Vista Commercial Hotel, Crewe, at eleven o'clock on a drizzling Sunday night, when God, Fred and I arrived. It had been a trying journey in a cold train, and all that saved me from pneumonia was the hot flush of embarrassment which stayed with me from the moment that God pulled a handful of brassières from his briefcase and gently handed one to me, saying, 'What do you think of that? Isn't it a beauty?' The man sitting next to me edged away noticeably, and the lady in the corner seat stood up, removed her luggage from the rack and left the compartment. God then asked me if I didn't think that the lining was the softest thing I had ever felt. He asked this in a loud clear voice, and the man sitting next to Fred leaned forward, unable to believe his luck. What a story he would have for the boys.

'He's a well known drag artist', Fred explained to him. 'The Yank is his manager.'

At the hotel, Fred and I had to share a double room, and God came in to talk to us. He began to explain our programme for the two days we would be in Crewe. As he talked, we unpacked. We washed and undressed, and God talked. We cleaned our teeth, and climbed into bed. God did not appear to notice. 'Goodnight, God', said Fred. 'Goodnight, God', I said. God said, 'Now, the important part of the whole deal is. . . .' Fred turned out the light. 'I guess you fellas want to get to bed', God said.

In the morning our four salesmen met us in the lounge, which we had hired for the day. There was Mr Thomas, the area salesman; Mr Ben Feather, the divisional sales manager; Mr Jim Pearce, the Northern regional sales manager; and John Angel. We all sat around the table, and poor Mr Thomas, the lowest rank present, was roundly abused by God, just to get us all into the right mood. Mr Feather was reprimanded for not keeping an eye on Mr Thomas. Mr Pearce was criticised for failing to notice that Mr Feather was not keeping an eye on Mr Thomas. John, the national sales manager, was mildly reminded that it was his job to make sure that Mr Pearce was watching Mr Feather watch Mr Thomas. Only I was praised, for having uncovered the dreadful secret of Crewe. I was not a popular sales controller at that moment.

'This is how we will work, fellas', God said. 'Where', he asked Mr Thomas, 'is your street map of Crewe?'

'I haven't got one', Mr Thomas confessed.

'What!' said God, astonishment wrinkling his kindly face, barely able to believe that anyone would venture from his home without his street map of Crewe. None of us had a street map of Crewe.

'I've got a picture of a dead horse', said Fred. This witticism earned him a long, hard look from God.

'A salesman must always carry a street map of every town on his territory', God said.

'You can't always get them', said Mr Feather, trying to cover up for his salesman.

'Of course you can get them', God roared. 'Even I, an American citizen, know where to get them. Go to the town hall and ask for a guide. They're up to their fannies in town guides. Go out and don't come back without one', he ordered the trembling Mr Thomas.

The map obtained, we marked on it in red ink every shop in Crewe that could conceivably sell brassières, from the list that I had compiled from the classified trades directory. There were thirty-five. 'We shall not leave this town until it is fully stocked, Titania-wise,' God promised, 'but first we shall call upon our one and only loyal stockist, who supported us with a full nine pounds worth of purchases last year. Lead us to it, Mr Thomas.'

In two cars we set out, jaws clenched and eyes coldly determined, for Mrs Porter's Wool Shop. We drove to a district which even the most optimistic estate agent could only describe as' ripe for development', and pulled up outside a half shop. God entered, followed by his six men.

It was a very narrow shop, dissected by a counter, and we filled it to capacity, crushed shoulder to shoulder. Mrs Porter, a thin lady striving to recapture her middle age, wore a hand-knitted jumper in apple green. Naked fear showed on her face.

'Good morning, madam', smiled God. 'Mrs Porter, I presume?'

Mrs Porter gulped visibly. 'If it's protection money you want,' she said, 'I've only got a little business. . . .' She thought we were the Mafia.

'Madam!' said God. 'I am the sales director of Titania Brassières. These are my colleagues. Surely you recognise Mr Thomas, our local representative?'

Mrs Porter adjusted her spectacles, and smiled with relief. God introduced us all, and we each shook the frail limp hand.

'We wish to thank you, Mrs Porter,' said God, 'for the support which you have given our company.'

'It's not much', she said, apologetically. 'I'm mostly wool. I only keep a few bras for my friends.'

'We are going to change all that for you, Mrs Porter', said God. 'This is your lucky day. We are going to make your business profitable. Do you know that you are our only stockist in Crewe?'

'Fancy that', Mrs Porter said, extreme anxiety in her eyes.

'Do you know what we are going to do for you, Mrs Porter? We are going to transform your shop into an emporium. The whole of Crewe will be struggling to get into your shop.'

'There's not much room', Mrs Porter said doubtfully. 'Besides, I was going to stop the brassières. It's too much worry. I'm only a woman on her own.'

The door opened, and two stout ladies entered. They tried to enter, that is. We had to shuffle along to make room for them. God, John and Mr Thomas had to move behind the counter. The rest of us huddled miserably at the end of the shop.

'Busy morning, is it, Mrs Porter?' asked the first lady.

'Oh no, Mrs Finigan. These gentlemen are from the brassières.'

'Who'd have thought it', Mrs Finigan said.

'Oh, you can't tell these days', said her friend. 'I've seen it, on the telly.'

Mrs Finigan wanted some more of the blue wool, and Mrs Porter had to squeeze past God and John and Mr Thomas. Mr Feather moved down behind the counter. Mrs Porter and Fred did a kind of samba, trying to avoid physical contact. 'Do you come here often?' asked Fred. 'I live here,' Mrs Porter said, puzzled, 'behind the shop.' 'Nice place you've got', Fred said conversationally, as he edged behind her.

76

Mrs Porter found the blue wool, but could not face the prospect of returning to her position behind the counter where five men now stood, so she tried to move to the front, but to my dismay a young woman entered the shop with two children, and we all just seized up, solid. Mrs Porter tried to reach Mrs Finigan, but tripped over Mr Thomas's sample case and fell into my arms.

'He's had it off', I heard Fred say from a distance. 'Who could have his luck!'

Quick as a flash, I made a decision. The only way to ease the crush was for me to stand on the counter. I leaped and got one leg up, but something was holding me back. Simultaneously came a muffled scream. It was Mrs Porter. In our collision, my blazer button had caught in her knitted jumper, and I had pulled it over her head.

Only vaguely do I recall the next moments. I remember my hand being slapped by Mrs Finigan as I tried to extricate myself; the two children and Mr Thomas bursting into tears; God shouting, 'Tell me what's going on, will ya?'; and Fred remarking to Mrs Finigan's friend, 'It's always these quiet ones you have to watch.' Then John took command. He squashed all Titania's contingent behind the counter, and personally served Mrs Finigan with a pair of size ten knitting needles. He then found a suitable pullover pattern for the woman with the children, and finally went into Mrs Porter's kitchen and made her and himself a cup of tea. When she was quite recovered from her unusual experience, God took over.

'What a lucky woman you are, Mrs Porter', he said. 'You will live to bless the day that Titania came to call. We will give you a range of the finest brassières sold in this country. We will advertise for you. You will make more money in a week than you now make in a month. Mr Thomas!' he called. 'Get some display material from your car. You and Mr Feather can set up a new window for Mrs Porter. Fred! Show Mrs Porter the advertisement we planned for her, and make out the contract. John! Get the sample case and show Mrs Porter our fastest selling lines. Mr Pearce! Bring your order pad. Gordon! Lock the door until Mrs Porter is through. We mustn't have anyone disturbing her.'

'Now,' said God, 'what I suggest is a three-dozen pack of our most popular brassière. . . .'

At the end of fifteen minutes Mrs Porter signed an order for thirty-dozen brassières, amounting to £275. Perhaps, I thought to myself, we *are* the Mafia.

The Wool Shop had certainly been transformed. Out from the window had come the knitting patterns, dozens of leaflets with photographs of gentlemen in woolly cardigans smoking pipes and holding fishing rods, ladies in twin-sets arranging flowers, and little boys in mufflers holding sailing boats. In went pink plastic bust forms, each wearing a bra taken from Mrs Porter's shelves, and Titania show cards of genteel ladies looking at their bosoms with scarcely concealed pride. Off the counter came the showcase of knitting needles, and on went a brass display stand, filled with what remained of the Wool Shop's meagre stock of brassières. Fred showed Mrs Porter the quarter-page advertisement which would appear in *The Crewe Courier* on Friday. He explained that Titania would pay half the cost of the ad, and gave a personal guarantee that the queue would start forming at seven o'clock on Saturday morning.

Our business now completed, we filed out of the Wool Shop. Mrs Porter stood numbly at the door. She said, 'But I don't really sell brassières.'

Fred said, quietly, 'You'd better start then, me old darling, or you won't be able to get in the shop.'

We returned to the Vista Commercial Hotel where God, elated by the success of the operation, bought us all a cup of coffee.

'Gordon,' he said, 'you have just witnessed as professional a piece of hard promotional selling as you are likely to see anywhere.'

'Congratulations', I said.

Over coffee, we discussed our next call, which we decided would be a large department store called Swansons. Mr Thomas told us that the buyer, whom he had never met, was a Miss Starkly—or was it Hagley? Mr Feather thought it was Mrs Teacher. I telephoned the store to enquire, and found that it was actually Miss Wiggins-Hope. All this led to an impromptu lecture by God on the importance of research into prospective accounts.

The attack on Miss Wiggins-Hope was carefully planned. Messrs Thomas, Feather and Pearce would form the vanguard, storm the corsetry department and pave the way for the heavy brigade. I hoped that Miss Wiggins-Hope would not be overwhelmed when Titania's top brass descended upon her without warning. She would have no chance.

Two by two we marched to Swansons, an impressive modern store. God said, 'This is us, fellas. This is the kinda place we must get in strong.'

Thomas and his two managers set off for the corsetry department, which was on the third floor, and after five minutes God said, 'They must have done the ground work by now. Let's go, fellas', and he stepped on the escalator, followed by John and Fred. I brought up the rear, feeling slightly superfluous, and I hung back, allowing a stranger, a well dressed man in a bowler hat, to go ahead of me. As I set foot on the long escalator leading to the third floor, I heard the disturbing sound of a lady in distress, and I saw Mr Thomas, Mr Feather and Mr Pearce coming down. The reason for this hurried retreat was the aristocratic-looking woman standing at the top, flapping her wrists with every appearance of agitation, and shouting, 'Get out of my department, get out, get out!' God reached the top and hesitated. 'Get out, get out!' Miss Wiggins-Hope screamed. God shrugged and descended. We passed when I was half-way up. 'Hello, God', I said.

'Hello, Gordon', he said.

John reached the top and came straight down again. He nodded in passing. Fred also turned and descended. 'Hello, Fred', I said. 'How's it going?'

'Can't complain', he said. 'Up and down.'

The stranger ahead of me reached the top. 'Get out!' ordered Miss Wiggins-Hope. He raised his hat, turned about smartly, and came down. I did not even look at Miss Wiggins-Hope, but stepped straight on to the down escalator.

We all gathered at the foot of the stairs. There were eight of us, including the man in the bowler hat. We smiled nervously at each other.

'My wife is waiting for me in the restaurant', he explained. 'I wonder how I can get word to her.'

'Carrier pigeon appears to be the only answer', Fred said.

We walked back to the Vista Commercial Hotel, a dejected group.

'What the hell did you guys say to Miss Wiggins-Hope to make her so mad?' God asked.

'All we did', said Mr Feather, 'was tell her that it was her lucky day. Titania, we said, would show her how to make greater profits. How could she hope, we asked, to run a successful department without Titania?'

'That's reasonable', God said. 'What did she say?'

'She said she had never been so insulted in her life. She said she had been in corsetry for twenty-seven years, and she knew how to run a successful department, and if we set foot in Swansons again she would send for the police.'

'What d'y'know', God said, shaking his head in perplexity.

A new plan was devised. God said that we should split up, perhaps seven was too many, and in any event he had shown us how things should be done, and in fact, when God, Fred and I left Crewe on Tuesday evening we were well satisfied with our results. Thirteen accounts had been opened for a total of just over one thousand pounds. No longer would Crewe be the poor relation of the brassière industry. John and Mr Pearce set off for Huddersfield, to start a similar saturation offensive. Mr Thomas was fired for incompetence.

Mr Feather was warned that divisional sales managers were two a penny, which probably gave him just the confidence he needed.

On Monday morning Fred came into my office and threw a copy of *The Crewe Courier* on my desk. 'Hot from the Press', he said.

Eagerly I opened it, and there, on page three, I found it; quarter-page, decorated with floating brassières and twinkling stars:

Titania brings Hollywood to Crewe!
Wear the Bras worn by the Stars!
Enter a new exotic world
at
Mrs Porter's Wool Shop,
8A, Gas Street,
Crewe.
'You will go far in y' .....
..... Titania'

'This will set the corsetry world by its ears', I said.

'I don't know about its ears', Fred said.

Inter-Branch Co-operation and the Knowledge Exchange System Internationally Applied

The Titania Brassière Company Ltd was the British branch of the American Titania International Inc., but our American parent company took little part in the day-to-day running of its offspring. Seventy-five per cent of the British company was owned by Galactic and World Distributors, and all that the New York office supplied was our styles and our sales director, Godfrey Barron. Nevertheless, there was some excitement at head office when one of our American bosses arrived, and a meeting of all our divisional sales managers was called for Saturday morning.

Mr Al Cony was due at ten o'clock, and God and I had spent an hour putting the finishing touches to the showroom where the meeting was to be held. My last task was to arrange the chairs in an accurate semicircle for the sales managers, and I carefully placed name cards on the seats. The boys arrived, disgruntled at having to work on Saturday morning. They were all neat in their navy blazers and striped Old Boys' ties. Reg sat straight down on Davis's name.

'Reg,' I said, 'you are sitting on Davis's chair.'

'Get stuffed', said Reg. I deduced that the mood of the meeting was going to be sensitive.

'That is no way to speak to your sales controller', I said.

'What are you going to do about it?' Reg said sourly.

'I shall see that Mr Al Cony is made aware that your division is bottom of the league in sales of Black Equalabra', I threatened.

80

'Furthermore, I shall ask you to give, before the assembled company, a sales pitch on the qualities of Mardi Bra—the festival in foamy lace.'

Reg moved with bad grace and sat on Eric's chair. I gave up. There was a strenuous morning ahead.

Everyone sat down. Ben sat on Laurie's chair, Bernard on Paul's, Davis on Ben's, Will on Reg's, Eric on Will's, Laurie on Davis's and Paul on mine, leaving me on Bernard's.

'Thank you all for your co-operation', I said. 'I shall remember this when I start on the sales statistics. Perchance you will regret this childish display of wilful insubordination.'

A wide variety of suggestions were hurled at me indiscriminately, until the door opened and God ushered in a bronzed, wrinkled man in a light-grey suit.

'Gentlemen,' said God, 'I have great pleasure in introducing Mr Al Cony, a Vice-President of Titania International.'

We all stood up and clapped politely, God leading the applause. Mr Al Cony said, 'Call me Al, fellas. When I say "Hi, fellas", I want you to say, "Hi, Al". OK?'

'OK', we said.

'Hi, fellas', said Al.

'Hi, Al', we said, raggedly.

'Louder', said Al.

'Hi, Al', we shouted.

Al walked up to Ben, shook his hand, picked up his name card and said, 'So you're Laurie, eh?'

'No, Al', said Ben. 'I'm Ben.' Al moved on, shook hands with Eric. 'You must be Will, eh?'

'No, Al', said Eric. 'I'm Eric.'

A shadow crossed Al's face. 'Who fixed these cards?' he asked.

'I did, Al', I confessed. He picked up my card. 'You're Bernard, eh?' he said.

'No, Al', I said. 'I'm Gordon.'

He looked at me hard. 'You work for CIA son?' he asked. God gave me a black look. I shrugged. It had taken me a long time to arrange this.

Al shook hands with the rest of us, and then walked to the centre of the room. In his thick Bronx accent he began to address us.

'Siddown', he said. We sat. 'I godda message from de president', he said.

'Not . . . not the president of the United States?' gasped Bernard, who was a fool who could not keep his mouth shut. Al turned to God. 'You got some real comedians here, Godfrey', he said. Then he shouted, 'No, not de president of de United States. Someone a

F

goddam more important to you an' me an' de whole goddam woild. De president of our company, Mr Irving Wolowicz, that's who!'

I let my jaw drop. Somehow I had to get back into Al's good books.

'De message is, listen fellas, de message is, "Open dem doors, and go, go go!" ' He glared at us. Eric paled visibly, and appeared to be trying to cover his Solihull Grammar School Old Boys' tie. Will stroked his silky moustache, frowning as though trying to absorb fully this gift from the all-highest.

Al suddenly pointed at me. 'What's de message, Jeffery?' he said.

'The message is,' I said, 'Open dem doors, Al, and go, go go!'

'Good boy, Jeffery', he said, and then turned sharply and flung out his arm at Davis, a nervous youth, who nearly fell backwards in terror. 'What's de message, sonny?' he bawled.

'Open those doors, sir, and go go, sir', poor Davis said in a high pitched Swansea singsong.

'Go, go, go', shouted Al. 'Now let us all say it together: open dem doors and go, go, go! Come on, fellas, shout it like you mean it.'

We began to shout in unison, 'Open dem doors, and go, go, go, open dem doors and go, go, go.' The rhythm crept into the blood. We could not stop. Reg rose, like a zombie, and pranced around the room, clapping his hands. Laurie stood up and clasped Reg's waist. Within seconds there was a long line of them, doing a conga around the showroom to the vibrant chant, 'Open dem doors and go, go, GO. . . .' Al was stamping his foot, flecks of foam at the corners of his mouth. God was banging two pink plastic bust forms together in strict tempo.

Mrs Tooks, the tea lady, put her head around the door. I was the only one still sitting down. 'Sir,' she said in her breathless voice, 'it's the phone, sir.' With relief I left the showroom and went into the main office. It was Miss Hacksey, the buyer from Barkings, the West End store.

'Yes, Miss Hacksey, what can I do for you?' I said. She was one of our biggest customers.

'I have a very special order', she said in her phoney Roedean. 'Please send me at once three twelfths style 946, Just Swell, 36B, in naughty nude, three twelfths 38C style. . . .' The door of the main office had burst open, and I could not hear a thing.

'Excuse me, Miss Hacksey,' I said, 'this is a bad line. . . .'

Al came up to me, looking flushed and happy. 'Who de goddam is it, Jeffery?' he asked.

'It's Miss Hacksey', I said, 'She . . .' Al pulled the phone from my hand. 'Hi, Miss Hacksey,' he bellowed, 'up your jacksey!' Then he put the receiver down. I was horror stricken, and tottered back to the

82

showroom. Gradually the noise subsided, and they all came back to join me.

'You miserable so-and-so', said Laurie. 'Why didn't you join in the fun? This Al is quite a character.'

'Yes?' I said. 'Do you know what he has just said to your best customer?' I told him. The blood drained from his face. 'You're kidding', he said. 'Not to Miss Hacksey. No one could say that to Miss Hacksey, she wouldn't allow it.'

'What's going on?' God said. I thought he was going to have a heart attack. 'Jee-zus,' he groaned, 'it cost me blood to open that account. Get her back on the phone and tell her it was a crossed line or something . . . anything. . . .'

I tried to get her, but she refused to speak to me. Laurie was moaning, 'This has cost me a thousand a year.'

'Still,' I told him, 'you had a good dance.'

Al called the meeting to order. We were a sorry lot. Laurie and God looked as miserable as sin; Bernard had a recurrence of his old back trouble; and Reg had strained his ankle. Al seemed quite unaware of the general spirit.

'Youse are a swell lotta guys', he said. 'When I get back Stateside I'll tell de president dat he has nuttin' to worry about over here. I'll tell him dat youse guys are goin' to get dem doors open. Can I give de president a message from London? Somet'in' that'll make him feel real good?'

Laurie, still in shock, gave him a message to take to the president, and was immediately fired. Reg tried to defend Laurie, and he was fired. I stood up.

'Siddown, Jeffery', snarled Al. 'You've caused anough trouble today'.

I sat down. Laurie and Reg prepared to leave. All the rest of the managers stood up, and Will said, 'If they go, we all go. We all resign.'

God was frantic, saying, 'Let's talk this over, boys, we can settle this, fellas', but Al said, 'Let 'em go, Godfrey. We can do better without dis crummy bunch of deadbeats.'

I must admit, I saved the day. It was pure inspiration, induced by the prospect of having to recruit an entirely new force of divisional sales managers. I could see those dingy hotel interview rooms in Birmingham, Leeds, Glasgow, taste the uncountable cups of bad coffee, foresee the inevitable query over my expenses. . . . All I did was shout, 'The Cock is open!' Everyone stopped what they were doing. Al thought I was insulting him in some way, and was just about to fire me and make a clean sweep, when God explained that The Cock was our local tavern.

We all trooped out. Within ten minutes Laurie and Reg had been reinstated. Within an hour Al had agreed to give the president Laurie's message, and suggested one or two piquant improvements. At two o'clock Al was carried back to the showroom paralytic, and God was trying to round up his sales managers who were dancing up Great Portland Street to the irresistible beat of the message.

No one ever discovered the meaning of the message. Al was never seen again, and God apologised for the fiasco, explaining that Al was the president's brother-in-law, who was regularly sent on overseas trips to keep him out of the way.

Still, as God said later, it does no harm to get an injection of American knowhow from time to time.

Financial Restructurisation and Group Capacity Assessment in Manufacturing/Sales Verticals

Mr McTavish was a brilliant businessman, the proud holder of eighty-seven directorships within the GAWD group, ranging from finance companies, through every conceivable form of textile manufacturing to gin distillers and travel agencies. Consequently, we at Titania did not see much of him. He appeared from time to time in order to refuse to sign cheques, and to veto any scheme which might require the spending of money, but on these occasions few of us saw more than a flash of his stern northern profile as he swept through the office. His beady eyes missed very little, however, and he could detect as if by magic the slightest sign of waste. I had suffered myself on more than one occasion. 'We are no' a bank', said Mr McTavish, his Glasgow accent always exaggerated when he was discussing economy, as he extracted a torn and out-of-date map from my waste-paper basket. 'I paid for it myself', I protested. 'It cost me a shilling, and I have had it for two years.'

'Then I hope you treat company property with more respect than you treat your own', he said. I believe that this example of flagrant extravagance on my part was mainly responsible for his rejection of my request for an increase in salary. Any man, he must have thought, who can throw away a map of south-west England when its coast line was still perfectly accurate, obviously has more money than he needs.

When Mr McTavish announced that in future he intended to make Titania's office his permanent headquarters, an atmosphere of gloom descended upon the staff. At a meeting of executives he told us that overheads were too high, and he would be introducing several essential economy measures during the coming weeks. To assist him, he had brought into the company a brilliant new accountant, whose progress within the GAWD group had been nothing short of aston-

84

ishing. Mr Foximan was to be given our complete co-operation, and with his help Titania would become an even more profitable company.

'Gentlemen,' concluded Mr McTavish, 'there will be no increases of salary for six months, and my office door is always open to anyone who can suggest ways and means of saving money.'

Mr Foximan was a very young man, and he spent a full thirty minutes talking to us until he was satisfied that he knew the brassière business intimately. We discovered that he was very highly qualified, being a nephew of GAWD's chairman's wife, and our respect for him grew even greater when he modestly recounted how he had reorganised his previous company by firing every member of the board of directors who was over thirty years of age.

For two weeks Mr McTavish and Mr Foximan were closeted together and we saw little of them. We waited in dread anticipation for the first cuts. I was chatting to the office manager when a sealed envelope was delivered to each member of the staff. Trying to control our trembling fingers, we opened our letters.

'With immediate effect', it said, 'all internal communications will be placed in brown envelopes. White envelopes will only be used for external letters.'

'Powerful,' said the office manager, 'and diabolically clever.'

'Staring us in the face,' I admitted, 'and it took an outsider to spot it.'

'Why do you suppose', said the office manager, 'that these internal communications were delivered to us sealed in white envelopes?'

'That's easy', I explained. 'They borrowed my secretary. Given a free hand, she could reduce Mr Paul Getty to penury.'

Fred Carter, who knew which side his bread was buttered, was seen making mysterious visits to Mr McTavish's office, sheets of paper in his hand. God was suspicious. 'That guy is up to something', he confided in me. In due course we discovered that Fred had been obtaining quotations from several manufacturers of plastic display material, and eventually succeeded in halving the cost of our plastic bust forms, of which we used thousands. Hundreds of pounds were saved, and Fred glowed in the warmth of Mr McTavish's congratulations. An unfortunate result of this economy, which naturally reduced the gauge and strength of the plastic used, was soon evident. Not one of the packages of bust forms despatched by our factory to customers and salesmen survived the handling of our carriers, but all were received in pieces. The loss to Titania was enormous. Gradually our name began to disappear from shop windows and counters. This, added to Fred's confidential assurances to Mr McTavish that we could safely reduce our advertising expenditure without affecting our sales, despite God's frantic denials, also effectively removed Titania's name from the public eye at the very time when our competitors were stepping up their advertising.

Mr Foximan had not been wasting his time. He produced a paper proving conclusively that we were carrying too much stock in our warehouse, and Mr McTavish was only too happy to agree. The factory was instructed to reduce production until our stock reached the figure recommended by Mr Foximan. The only way our factory could reduce production was by putting off staff, and a third of our machinists were sacked. It did not take long for the results to show: within weeks we began to run out of merchandise. Operating our type of saturation selling, with a large sales force calling frequently upon customers, it was necessary to hold large stocks so that orders could be despatched immediately. Any delay in sending out orders meant that on the salesman's next call he failed to obtain a new order because the previous one had not yet been received. Sales dropped, and salesmen became discontented because their commission also fell. When the error was recognised and the factory tried to re-engage staff, they could not be obtained.

Mr McTavish's refusal to increase overnight expenses for our salesmen meant that they could only afford to spend the night in the cheapest lodging houses, and therefore they drove home every night instead of staying away. The salesman increased his petrol expenditure and his driving time, and reduced his selling time, naturally reducing his sales and commission. The best of our salesmen quickly and easily found new jobs with companies who gave fair expenses, and preferred their salesmen to stay in decent hotels. The cost of replacing these salesmen was prodigious. There was the cost of advertising, interviewing, and training a new man. Most of all, there was the lost revenue from the vacant area for anything up to a month.

Our Mr Foximan was aghast at the staff we carried in the accounts department, and horrified at the number of girls in the sales department who operated the card index system. He persuaded Mr McTavish that a computer could do their jobs quicker, more efficiently and certainly more economically in the long run. A computer was installed, and our staff reduced very considerably. Mr McTavish was delighted with the results, and Mr Foximan bowed out of Titania to take a further step up the ladder, another feather in his cap. Unfortunately for the sales department, our new computer failed to give us the detailed information that we needed. It was not the computer's fault. Apart from frightening the occasional customer to death by sending out an invoice for £999,999, it did a great job on accounts. But it failed to tell us why Mrs Porter of The Wool Shop, Crewe, had not bought a brassière for six months, or how much business we had obtained in Bristol during July and August compared to the same period last year. The constant stream of information that we had been sending out to our salesmen and sales managers came to an abrupt halt, and sales suffered accordingly.

Thus, the inspired work of our business genius Mr McTavish had one vitally important and lasting effect. Titania fairly rapidly dropped from No. 1 in the brassière business to become one of the run-of-the-mill firms hovering around No. 15. Today, Titania is a little known company with a small sales force, a minute advertising budget, and a factory giving most of its production to other more successful companies. God has gone, a heart-broken man. Fred Carter remains, the supremo.

But credit where it is due. We did reduce overheads.

Chapter 8

Reciprocity in the Line Management Environment

There is a moment in every successful businessman's life when he suddenly realises that the breakthrough has occurred; the summit, however far, is in view, and mentally he leaves the ranks of the workers and joins the bosses. I experienced such an emotion when Mr McTavish appointed me General Manager of Edgar Pile (Southend) Ltd, a sportswear manufacturing company recently swallowed up by Galactic and World Distributors. It was a habit of GAWD's to take over smaller firms, dispose of many of the old management and replace them with employees of the group, and thus Mr McTavish achieved his eighty-eighth directorship and I received the promotion I so richly deserved.

'This is your big chance', Mr McTavish told me. 'Turn last year's loss into a profit, and you will become one of GAWD's chosen people, part of that exclusive team of young management experts who will eventually control our great organisation.'

This was the sort of thing I had in mind, but there were answers that my restless, questing mind demanded.

'Will I get a salary increase?' I asked.

'Not yet', Mr McTavish said.

'Can I have a company car?'

'No', Mr McTavish said.

'How much did Edgar Pile lose last year?'

'Forty-four thousand pounds', said Mr McTavish.

Mentally I rejoined the workers.

'Remember', he said, 'that this will be YOUR company. RE-build it, remould it, do with it what you will, so long as it makes a profit. I shall not interfere, but leave you a completely free hand, understand? You will not spend any money, of course, without my permission, and you will not authorise any wage increases for your staff. Expenses and petty cash will be checked weekly by the company accountant. A weekly report on sales intake, invoice values and production statistics must be on my desk each Friday afternoon at five o'clock, and I shall expect a telephone call from you each evening at . . .', he checked a cheap plastic diary carefully, 'approximately seven thirty-six. Your immediate superior, apart from me, is Miss Pile, the only one of the original directors whom we have retained.'

'Miss Pile?' I said, with interest. 'I've never worked for a woman before.'

'I have, for years', said Mr McTavish. 'Mrs McTavish. It is not always easy.'

It was the first joke I had ever heard him make, and I laughed until I saw his face and realised that it was not a joke. I had no fears about having a woman boss, because my business experience had taught me that women in responsible jobs were coolly efficient and hard working, and at least as reliable as their male counterparts.

I met Miss Pile in our Bond Street showroom, where she had her office. She was a gracious lady, desperately fighting her fortieth birthday, not altogether unsuccessfully. She was jumpy with nervous energy, and distant, until she realised that I was prepared to be friendly, and then she thawed charmingly and deliberately, and I could see what I was up against.

Miss Pile told me that the firm had been highly successful until the death of her father, since when she had found the task of running the company increasingly difficult until it was forced into liquidation. GAWD had bought it from the liquidator, chiefly for its tax loss, and she was full of hope that her father's firm would now begin to flourish again. I assured her that it would, and she smiled at me meltingly and touched my hand, and said that I should call her Felicity.

We then went to the factory, some miles away, and after a guided tour she led me into a small shabby room.

'This was my father's office', she said. 'I would like it to be yours. Daddy died in this room, on the chair you are sitting on.' I jumped up, surreptitiously brushing the seat of my trousers.

'I shall be honoured to use this office, Felicity', I said. She was near to tears, and she touched my hand again.

'If you need him,' she said, 'Daddy will help you.'

'How kind', I murmured.

'Daddy is just behind you', she said. I whirled round, an icy hand clutching my heart, but it was only a photograph on the wall of a stern looking gentleman in a winged collar. Respectfully, I nodded at the late Mr Pile.

'Together', said Felicity, 'we shall build a great business again. With my designing and selling, and my loyal staff, and my wonderful friends and contacts who will support me, and with your, er, whatever-it-is. . . .'

'Administrative ability?' I suggested.

'Yes, that's it, we cannot fail.'

'Plus GAWD's money', I said.

'Don't tell me that you too think only of money, like that awful Mr McTavish', she said.

'It's useful in running a business, Felicity', I said.

'I agree up to a point,' she said, 'but first comes integrity, honesty and truth.'

I was unable to answer, rarely having come across these vital commodities in my varied business career, but I was willing to give them a whirl.

Specific Deployment of Non-Cybernetic Strategy

Those of us who are addicted to the financial pages are well acquainted with board-room strife. We watch with amusement the acrimonious accusations, the crafty manoeuvring and the blatant wooing of shareholders. Miss Pile, without allies and against overwhelming odds, made a unique contribution to board-room history, and gained my respect and admiration for the female as a top executive.

At the first official meeting of directors, Mr McTavish announced for the record that he was managing director of Edgar Pile (Southend) Ltd. He was taken unawares when Miss Pile opposed this decision, and demanded that she be appointed managing director.

'I am managing director', Mr McTavish stated, amazed that anyone should question this elementary fact. 'You, Miss Pile, are the sales director.'

Miss Pile then began to weep. No further business could be done, and the meeting was adjourned. Miss Pile allowed me to buy her a brandy.

Next day there was another meeting, at which Miss Pile wept from beginning until its premature abandonment. Mr McTavish was becoming rattled. He had never met this situation before.

At the next meeting, he gave in. With a Scottish exclamation of extreme feeling, he said, 'All right, all right Miss Pile. You can be managing director.' Miss Pile stopped weeping immediately and made a short, gracious speech of acceptance, expressing gratitude at the faith her fellow directors had in her, and demanding their fullest co-operation in the difficult task before her. Sweetly she asked Mr McTavish to vacate his chair so that she could take her seat at the head of the table, and like a man in a dream he did so, muttering audibly, 'It doesn'a mean a thing, the silly woman.'

The Interfaced Distribution Vectors of Stock Control

My first action in my new job was to take stock of the factory contents, and I was staggered at the large quantity of materials in the stock-room. A quick valuation showed that we could recoup the entire cost of the purchase of the company by making up and selling these expensive fabrics, and this we did, until all that was left of the old stock was seven hundred yards of a man-made jersey called 'Synthelon'.

'We must get rid of this jersey, Felicity', I said. 'Make some new samples and I will cost them at a written-down value of the cloth. You can offer them to Mrs Herring.'

Mrs Herring was the buyer for Maisiemode, a huge chain of nationwide fashion shops owned by GAWD. This was a chance to dispose of our Synthelon jersey and do some satisfactory vertical business within the GAWD group.

Miss Pile returned from her meeting with Mrs Herring in triumph. She flopped down in my office, worn out, while her secretary struggled in with the sample case.

'Congratulate me!' she said gaily. 'Your own little managing director, wearing her sales director's hat, has brought you an order for over ten thousand pounds!'

'Felicity,' I said, 'this is a magnificent order, but you have sold fifteen thousand yards of Synthelon jersey, in eight colours. We have in stock seven hundred yards, in brown and grey. You haven't sold any brown or grey at all.'

'Mrs Herring doesn't like brown, and she thinks grey is unlucky', Miss Pile said.

'It's unlucky for me', I said. 'The object of this exercise was to sell off our stock. You haven't sold a yard of it. Also, I priced these blouses very low because the stock was old. I shall never buy more at this price. And the delivery date!' I almost cried. 'Three weeks! You know that it would take us a month to make this order, even if we had the material in stock. We just cannot do it, Felicity.'

'Miss Pile, please', she said coldly. 'Am I to understand that you refuse to make this order on which I worked so hard?'

'That is exactly what you are to understand', I said.

'Then I shall inform the chairman of GAWD, whom I know socially, that my general manager is incompetent as well as insubordinate.'

'At least', I said, 'tell the buyer of Maisiemodes that a three week delivery is impossible.'

'You tell her', said Miss Pile. 'I cannot be expected to run the firm single-handed.'

I telephoned the jersey manufacturer to place my order. I was given a three months delivery date. I telephoned another manufacturer. They had discontinued that particular jersey. There was no demand for it, they said. I telephoned ten manufacturers. The jersey was unobtainable. I telephoned Mr McTavish. He said he had troubles of his own.

The next day I went to see Mrs Herring, and told her that there would be a slight delay in the delivery of her blouses. How much delay, she asked. At least a month, I said. She screamed at me that unless she had the order in full within three weeks she would report me to her boss, who was a personal friend of the chairman of GAWD. Everyone was a friend of the chairman but me, and my prospects of ever achieving his friendship were receding hourly.

For two weeks I searched for Synthelon jersey. It had disappeared from the face of the earth. Miss Pile refused to speak to me, but sent messages through her secretary expressing her extreme displeasure.

Mrs Herring phoned me daily to scream at me. I began to dream about Synthelon jersey, great masses of it, oozing around my ears until it finally buried me. Then the dreams stopped, but only because I stopped sleeping.

Idly glancing through the *Drapers' Record*, looking for suitable employment for cashiered general managers, I saw in the obituary column the news of the sad demise of a Mr Angus Bruce Farquhar, aged ninety-four, the ex-owner of Dumfries and Farquhar Ltd, a textile company in Wigtonshire, Scotland. It was possibly the only one in Great Britain that I had not telephoned. I found their number, and spoke to the sales manager. 'You do not, of course, manufacture plain Synthelon jersey?' I asked him.

'No', he said. 'We used to, but there is no demand for it.'

'There is a bloody demand for it', I said. 'I want it.'

'Well, we have substantial stocks here', he said, and his description matched my requirements exactly. We sobbed at each other in excitement as I placed my order.

'Before I can despatch such a large order,' he said, 'could you please give me some trade references? Frankly, I have never heard of your firm.'

'I've never heard of yours either,' I told him, 'but you need have no worries. We are a subsidiary of GAWD.'

There was a moment's silence at the other end. Then he said, 'So are we.'

'If you want confirmation,' I said, my head swimming with disbelief, 'contact Mr McTavish, at GAWD House.'

'I know him well', he said. 'He is a director of this company.'. .

I quickly spread the good news. Miss Pile spoke to me at last. Mr McTavish said, 'I forgot about Dumfries and Farquhar.'

Miss Pile came to see me at the factory. 'It's nice to see you again, Miss Pile', I said.

'Felicity please', she smiled touching my hand.

It came to pass that the firm of Edgar Pile (Southend) Ltd began to prosper, and within a few short months we had a factory working to capacity, and a full order book. Felicity Pile knew what her customers wanted, and she had the brazen nerve to sell at prices so outrageously high that I found it difficult to watch her. Her relationship with her customers, who were the cream of the retail trade, was gushingly informal. She could sell best of all to those who also had pretensions to high social standing, and the gossip in her showroom when she was entertaining a buyer was straight out of 'Lady Dorothy's Diary'. Yet she was no fool, and when the kissing and the chit-chat ended, Felicity usually had an order worth hundreds of pounds. Even Mr McTavish had to admit that she was a valuable asset to the company, provided she was not allowed to purchase or entertain indiscriminately, because like so many women in the fashion industry, her talent and hard work were liable to be destroyed by her inability to understand the economics of the business. This was the reason for her disaster when she took over the firm on the death of her father, as the records proved. It was commonplace for her to take an order for a hundred pounds, and then spend twenty pounds taking her buyer to dinner, completely dissipating her profit. Basically, she felt that it was not quite respectable to be in commerce, and after a hard selling session she had to soften her image by a great show of extravagance.

She and I swung from the coldest hostility to the warmest friendship but the friendliness would evaporate instantaneously whenever I opposed her.

I happened to be in her office during a cold war period, and as she was temporarily absent, I answered her telephone when it rang. It was a customer with certain instructions regarding a delivery, and I sat at her desk to take notes. Looking up, I saw her enter the room, her icy mask on. She addressed her secretary, who had a desk in a corner of the room. 'Louise,' she said, 'tell the general manager that he happens to be sitting in my chair.'

Louise, a dark, intense girl, sat up, a glint of interest appearing in her eye. 'Sir,' she said, 'you are sitting in Miss Pile's chair.'

'It's all right, Felicity', I said. 'I was just taking some . . .'

'Kindly inform the gentleman that my name is Miss Pile', she said.

'Miss Pile's name, sir, is Miss Pile', said Louise.

'Tell Miss Pile, Louise,' I said, 'that this is neither the time nor the place for intimate revelations of a sensational nature.'

The message was passed, with due solemnity.

'Insubordination,' said Miss Pile, 'I will not stand. Tell him.'

'Insubordination Miss Pile will not stand', said Louise.

'Tell him', said Miss Pile, bringing up the big guns, 'that he is sitting in MY FATHER'S CHAIR, and he is to vacate it immediately.'

We faced each other across the desk, one yard apart, seething. It was my turn now, but I could think of nothing to say. Louise was waiting, tense and receptive. I hated to let her down.

'Tell Miss Pile', I said, slowly, in case inspiration suddenly came to me, 'that I can't think of anything to say.'

'The general manager', said Louise slowly, 'says he can't think of anything to say.'

'Yes I can!' I said.

'Yes he can, Miss Pile.'

'Tell her, Louise, plainly and clearly, that I am fed up to the back teeth with her tantrums, and that she is the stupidest woman I have ever known—spoilt, snobbish and phoney—and she can now have her chair back, and she also has a new vacancy in her firm—to wit, general manager.'

'He says you can have your chair back, Miss Pile', said Louise, found wanting in the final analysis.

Chapter 9

I was thinking to myself that I had had as versatile and practical a business training as it was possible to obtain. I had worked for myself, for a small company, and for a massive company. I had sales experience with the wholesale and the retail trade, and also with the general public. Production; personnel control; management. Mistakes I had made, but lessons I had learned. I was really a valuable property, stuffed with knowledge and experience, and worth a fortune to the right firm, I was thinking, as I made my way to the labour exchange.

The clerk was very helpful. I explained my position, and told him my history. He listened and took notes, and then thumbed through a collection of dog-eared cards.

'Ever done any paint spraying?' he asked.

'Not deliberately', I said.

'I have a vacancy here for a heating closer. Ever done it?'

'Quite likely', I said. 'What is it?'

'I dunno. No one seems to know. Had it on the card for two years.'

'Doesn't sound like me', I said. 'Anything else?'

'Erection?'

I shrugged modestly.

'Steel erection, I mean.'

'No.'

'Can't understand a feller like you being without a job. You could do anything. You could be a consultant, with your experience of management.'

A Management Consultant! That was it! Why had it not occurred to me before? I went straight to the public library and took out two books on Management Consultancy which I read, one after the other. They were not easy to read, because I kept falling asleep, but they left me in no doubt as to my future. They were filled with the same problems, with the same solutions, that I had so often encountered, but how exciting they became when couched in the exotic phrases of Management Consultancy. Activity sampling, variety reduction, ergonomics, regression analysis. Fantastic!

Take 'needs analysis', for example: 'comparing the skills and knowledge required to do a job effectively with the skills and knowledge of the individual who is doing the job'. True original thinking there, all right. And the brilliance of 'exponential smoothing' left me gasping. 'A technique for judging future demand by taking into consideration demand in the past.' Incredible! But even more startling: 'the more up-to-date the statistics, the more relevant they may be to the future'.

I was lost in admiration for Management Consultants, and the contribution they were making to present day business thinking. This was for me.

I wrote out a tasteful, low cost-space ratio advertisement: 'Free-lance Management Consultant now available for business assignment.' It went into *The Daily Telegraph* and brought me a shoal of replies.

Most of my correspondents assumed that I had money to invest. I was offered a Generalship in a firm selling cosmetics direct to the public for a mere three thousand pounds. All I had to do was recruit an army of corporals, sergeants, captains and majors, and I would almost get my money back. I wrote a polite letter to them saying that if I were capable of raising such an army, I would find it more profitable to take over the Argentine. I was also offered launderettes, vending machine territories, and membership of an exclusive syndicate offering 100 per cent monthly on my money were I to invest it in a unique and unbeatable roulette system.

Then there was a letter from a firm called Atomic Reading, requesting me to make an appointment at my earliest convenience with a Mr Bob Bishop.

Atomic Reading had splendid offices in Bloomsbury, furnished throughout in the finest fibreglass and hardboard. Mr Bishop was a youthful fresh-faced American of such transparent honesty and sincerity that I immediately took to him. His quiet, educated drawl and charming manners were Ivy League standard, vastly different from the transatlantic gentleman of Titania Brassières.

'It was good of you to come', he said, with a flash of American dentistry at its most expensive, as he led me into a large white office and settled me into a comfortable chair. 'Are you acquainted with our Atomic Reading organisation?'

'I regret I am not', I said. 'It appears to be some kind of educational establishment.'

'Indeed it is, sir. That is exactly what it is. We teach people to read,' he smiled, and I blinked, temporarily blinded by the glare, 'but with a difference. We teach people how to read faster. Do you know how fast you read?'

'Pretty fast', I said.

'Permit me to contradict you', he said. 'You read pretty slowly. We have our own method of discovering how fast you read. We let you

96

read for five minutes, then we count the words and divide by five. This gives us your words-per-minute rating.'

'Ingenious', I said. 'The finest brains in Management Consultancy could not have devised a more efficient method.'

He graciously acknowledged my compliment. 'You read, I guess, at a rate not exceeding two hundred and fifty words per minute. What would you say if I told you that Atomic Reading could increase your rate, not two-fold, not even three-fold, but a minimum of four-fold? And, if you are a good student, perhaps ten-fold?'

'I should be astonished', I said.

'Well, sir, I can show you positive proof that we have students of Atomic Reading who can read at the rate of five thousand words per minute. Think of it. Hamlet in seven minutes. The complete works of Shakespeare in three hours ten minutes.'

'Including the sonnets?' I asked.

'Including the sonnets', he affirmed, '*and The Rape of Lucrece.*'

'Unbelievable', I said.

'You realise what this means to students, businessmen, politicians, and everyone who has to get through a lot of reading. Such people spend so much time studying reports and reading essential matter, that they have little time to get to grips with the real problems of their work. Atomic Reading gives them greater knowledge, greater achievement and more leisure. This is what I have to sell. What do you think?'

'I think, Mr Bishop, that if your claims are accurate, you have much to give the world. Is Atomic Reading your own idea?'

'I guess that it is, mostly', he said. 'There are other methods in the States, but Atomic Reading is the result of many, many years of research on my part.'

'May I congratulate you,' I said. 'But where do I come in? As a Management Consultant, how can I help you?'

'Let me tell you my plans, Mr Bennett—perhaps you will permit me to call you Gordon? Call me Bob, everybody does—and I hope you find them interesting. Atomic Reading now has four schools established in the United Kingdom, and they are beginning to take off. Some weeks ago I opened a school in Amsterdam, and the results have been beyond my expectations. My plans now are to open up the continent of Europe to Atomic. I want schools in Holland, Belgium, France and Germany. There is nothing to stop us.'

'You are well financed then, Bob', I said.

'Gordon, if I told you who was behind us, you would fall flat on your face. Money is no object, we can go right ahead and expand. Except for one thing. Management. I can personally control the British schools, and I can find managers to run each of the continental establishments, but there must be an overall controller there, someone I can trust to look after my foreign interests. That is why I wrote to you. There is a fortune in this for somebody who is prepared to live on the continent, open schools for me, staff them, guide them. Five schools this year, twenty next year, fifty the following year, and who knows after that? Russia? India? China? How does it appeal?'

'It appeals, Bob', I said.

'Right. Then tell me about yourself. What experience do you have that makes you think that you can tackle this enormous job that could make you a wealthy man in a few short years?'

Briefly I told him. I explained how I had built up a great catering concern until forced out of business by my only real rival, Sir Charles Forte. I told him how I had been the one to introduce margarine with ten per cent added butter into the nation, until Van den Bergh had stopped my supplies, fearing that I was becoming too powerful. I went into no real details about the way I had almost revitalised the men's tailoring business, bringing in a brand new fashion that might have swept the world but for the vicious campaign waged against me by the *Tailor and Cutter*. I touched briefly on my board-room experiences in the fashion industry, but dwelt nostalgically on my original and revolutionary statistical research into the corsetry business. I related how I had run Galactic and World Distributors almost single-handed, until sickened by the unnecessary extravagance and reckless expenditure of money amongst its top management.

Bob Bishop listened to me intently, his eyes closed for greater concentration. He was silent for almost a minute after I finished my saga, and then he sat up with a jerk and said, 'That's just great, Gordon, I guess we are in business.' We beamed at each other in mutual admiration.

The Educationalist in Business. Audio-Induction Factorisation

If I had my time over again, I used to think, I would choose the academic life. The sheltered existence of the cloisters, and the true satisfaction of helping to educate and civilise the masses would be my aim, and now it appeared that my dreams had materialised. I was even more convinced of my good fortune when I attended an Atomic Reading demonstration. Only fourteen people turned up, but they were a truly representative collection, including a journalist, a barrister, a student, a secretary, a children's nurse and a publisher. Bob Bishop began his talk, after welcoming them in tones so cultured and restrained that they were all put at their ease.

'Atomic Reading is the greatest educational breakthrough of the

98

century', he told us sincerely. 'In every field of learning we can continue our studies through a lifetime, never ceasing to gather greater knowledge. Only in the art of reading, the source of most of our knowledge, do we fail to progress. We are taught to read at the age of five, and once we have grasped the function, our tuition ends. We practise, we enlarge our vocabulary, but basically there is nothing further that our teachers can tell us. In what other field of learning, ladies and gentlemen, do we complete our studies at such an early age?'

'Toilet training?' suggested the children's nurse.

'Some of us, madam, never stop learning', said Bob, with a flash and a grin that certainly won over the three ladies in the audience, even if it lost the journalist.

'It is an established medical fact', went on Bob, 'that we use only a tiny part of our brain. Ten per cent is the figure that I have been given, although I cannot vouch for its accuracy. What we do know is that the wonderful human brain is capable of so much more than the meagre exercise that we give it. Why does the brain hit a blank wall when it comes to reading? It is because when we read we say the words to ourselves, or sub-vocalise, therefore we read only as fast as we speak. Imagine what happens when the printed word is transmitted directly to the brain, as happens when we look at a picture. Take the print on the wall. You do not look at it and say, "There is a boat, and then a man, and then a child, and then a beachball." You look at it and you know at a glance that there is a picture of a seashore. This is how Atomic Reading works. First we teach you to absorb phrase by phrase, then line by line, then paragraph by paragraph, until eventually our aim is page by page. Yes, ladies and gentlemen, that is what our human brain can do: absorb an entire page of print, with total comprehension, just as it can look at a picture, or a street scene, or a football match, and immediately respond to its meaning. I do not promise that you will ever reach this standard. Your children might, or their children, when Atomic Reading becomes generally accepted by educational authorities, but I can promise you that your reading speed will triple or quadruple within the short eight-week course that we offer you.'

He stopped and introduced us to an instructor, a casually dressed girl, who borrowed a book from a member of the audience, bent it back until its spine creaked, to the agitation of the owner, placed it before her on a table and began to turn the pages, running her fingers over the print in a zig-zag. At the end of ten minutes she was stopped, and we found that she had read about eleven thousand words. She then gave us a précis of what she had read, leaving us in little doubt that she had understood and remembered most of it.

Bob addressed us again. I expected some hard selling, but there was none. 'The price of our course, ladies and gentlemen, is fifty-five pounds. You may think this is high, but it is nothing in comparison with what you will gain. You are invited to stay for refreshments, and ask as many questions as you wish of my staff and myself. If you decide to take the course, it will be necessary for you to leave a deposit of a minimum of five pounds in order to reserve a place in one of our ten classes which start next week, and which are rapidly filling up.'

Four people joined, one paying in full. Most of the others were undecided, and only one person left at once, obviously unimpressed.

Bob and I went back to his office. 'I had better take a course as soon as possible', I said.

'Sure,' he said, 'if you want to.'

'But isn't it vital for me to read Atomically?' I asked.

'I suppose so', he said. 'I'll give you a big discount. Tell you what, just slip me a tenner and I'll get you on a course for free.'

I was outraged, but Bob laughed. 'Just testing you, kid', he said.

'Anyway,' I told him, 'we have not yet discussed my fees for this international operation.'

'I've been thinking about it', he said, 'and I have a surprise for you. We shall not pay you a fee.'

'That is a surprise', I admitted.

'What I intend to offer you, if I get the agreement of my board, is 10 per cent of the net profit of each school you open. I figure it this way: our aim is 100 students enrolled each month, giving a gross monthly income per school of £5,500. Advertising costs will be, say, £1,000, staff salaries another £1,000, rent and other general running costs about £500. Monthly profit per school, £3,000 gross, say £2,000 net. You should make £200 per school per month. At the end of the first year, you should make £1,000 a month. At the end of the second year, maybe £3,000 a month. After four years, say £8,000 a month. I am speaking conservatively, of course. No point in making unrealistic promises. How does it grab you?'

'I could manage', I said.

'We shall naturally give you a draw against your earnings for the first month or two, if you require it.'

'I shall require it', I said firmly.

'Agreed then', said Bob, holding out his hand for me to shake. 'Once the board have confirmed these arrangements, I shall have a contract drawn up. When can you start?'

'I have several personal and business matters to settle,' I said, 'and arrangements to be made with my bank. I'll start tomorrow.'

Atomic Reading actually worked. Admittedly, it was a great

100

strain on the eyes, but I was assured that this would pass when I became more proficient. My headache, too, would go in time, and I was, after all, trying to squeeze an eight-week course into two weeks. I found that I was able to read a newspaper in three minutes, although if there was anything interesting in it, I had to read it again in the pre-Atomic way. I ignored the odd looks I received in the tube, as my hands moved quickly over the pages of my book, and once, when I was standing, a girl offered me her seat, under the impression that I was reading braille.

I was passed out at a private session by the chief instructor, with a reading speed of 880 words per minute, and they gave me a certificate. Bob said he would have it framed for me, and he was as good as his word. In fact, he was better than his word, because when my diploma was returned to me, my reading speed stated 3,880 words per minute. Bob also signed the certificate, which tended to reduce the effect, because his writing was that of a backward twelve year old. Perhaps, I thought, they did not set much store in handwriting at Harvard, where, Bob told me, he had spent three brilliant years.

The Uni-Angloid in the Multi-Lingual Environment. The Marketing of the Abstract Durable

Bob Bishop and I arrived in Amsterdam and went straight to the Hilton Hotel where a suite had been booked for Bob, and an adjoining room for me.

We then took a taxi to the Atomic Reading Institute in Keizergracht, a charming canal street, and I was immediately impressed by its quiet air of scholarship. The school was a replica of the one in London, but it was tidier and whiter, and the staff spoke better English. Bob introduced me to the principal, a tall, grave Dutchman named Klein who looked every inch a professor.

'Mr Gordon Bennett is my personal representative in Europe', Bob told Mr Klein. 'He has spent two years in the United States studying Atomic Reading, and has lectured at most of our important universities. He has demonstrated his phenomenal reading speed to a congressional committee on education, who have since recommended that Atomic Reading should be introduced into the American educational system. I want you to give him every assistance, Mr Klein.'

'It will be an honour and a privilege, sir', Mr Klein said, looking at me with a mixture of fear and wonder.

It was with a similar mixture that I looked at Bob when Mr Klein left the room. 'Why did you say that?' I said.

'By the time he finds out the truth', Bob said, 'you won't need him any more.'

'But that is no way to treat an honourable man and a scholar', I protested. 'Suppose he realises that you have lied to him and resigns. Where will you find another principal of his calibre?'

'The same way I found him', Bob said. 'He answered our advertisement a couple of months ago. He was an assistant in a sex shop.'

Bob said that he had to return to the Hilton, where he had an important appointment. I stayed at the school to examine their accounts and enrolment figures, and I could see that business was not as good as Bob had indicated. Enrolments were being made at the rate of only forty a month, and many students were behind with their payments. The bank statement showed a balance of 264 guilders, not enough to pay for our rooms at the Hilton, and the giro account was not much better. I made notes, intending to have a serious talk with Bob.

A demonstration was due to start at six o'clock in the afternoon, and I sat in reception to count the people arriving. It was quite encouraging. Our audience began to arrive at half past five, and there were twenty-five sitting down when Klein began to address them in a confident and confidential manner, which he must have picked up from the sex business. The Dutch language, they say, is a difficult language to learn, and I would go along with that statement. I would go further and say that it is a difficult language to listen to. I found that I had to keep clearing my throat in sympathy with the speakers.

Mr Klein suddenly broke into English. 'Ladies and gentlemen', he said, and his audience did not turn a hair at the change of language, 'I am proud to introduce to you Mr Bennett, who has come from America to talk to us. Mr Bennett knows more about Atomic Reading than any living person. He reads at five thousand words a minute, which he will demonstrate to us.'

Everyone turned to look at me. They saw a man with a chalk-white face, whose heart had stopped beating, but whose sweat glands had gone mad.

'Mr Bennett has instructed the American Senate in the art of Atomic Reading, and one of his most successful pupils is the president of the United States', said Mr Klein. A scattering of applause came from the older members of the gathering, but the younger ones stared at me belligerently. A youth with almost waist length hair hissed, 'Get out of Vietnam.' Outnumbered as I was, I agreed.

'Does any person have a book for Mr Bennett to demonstrate with?' asked Mr Klein. A book was produced and handed to me. *Als je een meisje bent*, it was called, and it took me thirty seconds to read the title, which worked out at ten words a minute.

'I do not read Dutch well', I mumbled.

'Does any person have an English book?' asked Mr Klein, and

102

another volume was offered to me. It was *History of Western Philosophy*, by Bertrand Russell.

'I cannot use this book', I said. 'It would be unfair. I have already read it. I should be deceiving you.'

'The fair play of the Englishman is well known in Holland', said Mr Klein, and personally led another round of applause. Meanwhile I was trying to induce a small heart attack, nothing serious, just something to put me out of action for an hour.

'Here is an English newspaper', somebody said, and he held up a copy of the *Daily Express* which I had bought at London Airport and had thoroughly digested. I walked to the front of the room, and laid the paper flat on a table.

'I shall not read the front page, because it contains news which I may have heard during the day', I said. 'I shall turn to the back page, which apparently contains . . .' I peered at it, puzzlement spreading across my face, '. . . information concerning sporting events. Uninteresting as it may be to you all, as well as to me, I shall endeavour to demonstrate Atomic Reading, to prove that speed is compatible with full comprehension.'

There was silence in the room as I sat down, cracking my knuckles and settling myself comfortably after the style of a concert pianist.

'Start timing, Mr Klein,' I said, 'NOW!'

I placed my right index finger at the top left-hand corner of the sports page, and moved it swiftly across the paper, left to right, to left and right, zig-zagging down to the bottom right hand corner. 'Finished!' I called out. There was a gasp from the onlookers. 'Five and fifty seconds', shouted Mr Klein exultantly.

I handed the newspaper to a lady in the front row. Several people gathered behind her, reading over her shoulder.

'You must forgive me if I do not get everything exactly correct', I said. 'I know nothing about sport, apart from chess. . . .' I sat back in my chair, took a deep breath, and began.

'It appears', I said, 'that there is a football team called Nottingham Forest, who wish to sell one of their players. Several other football teams are interested in purchasing this gentleman, a certain Joe Giggleswick, including Tottenham, Liverpool and Coventry. . . .' I recited the rest of the article, as I had remembered it from my close perusal a few hours ago.

'At the Manor Place Baths', I continued, 'Eric Kid Johnson knocked out Paddy "Bignose" Connor in the third round. . . . The English rugby team were narrowly beaten by Wales 24–6. Tries were scored by D. Jones, E. Jones, F. Jones and G. Jones. . . . At a place called Kempton Park yesterday, the two-thirty race was won by Little Knob at 2–1, ridden by a certain L. Piggott. The winner was napped, whatever that means, by The Scout, whoever that is. The three o'clock was won by. . . .'

'I think we have heard enough, Mr Bennett sir', said Mr Klein, beaming, and I received my third round of applause that day. A gentleman who announced that he was Mr Verdonk shook hands with me and begged to be allowed to join the course. I graciously accepted him as a student. A further twelve people signed up, and another six promised to return with their money the next day. It was, Mr Klein told me, the most successful demonstration ever held.

Glowing with glory, I went back to the Hilton to tell Bob Bishop how I had helped to bring a little extra light into the lives of some Amsterdam citizens. I knocked at Bob's door and walked in, to discover that he too was doing his best for the local citizenry. He was in bed with two of them, and although I was shocked there was some measure of relief that they were both young ladies.

'I've been doing some work for you', Bob said. 'Two new students, Marga and Sonia.'

'How do you do', I said, opening my brief case and bringing out a couple of application forms. 'If you would kindly complete these. . . .'

'I have no pen with me', said Marga or Sonia.

'If you care to join us', said Bob, 'we can have a grand enrolling session.'

New as I was in the educational field, I instinctively knew that it was bad for discipline for a school official to have too intimate a relationship with his pupils, so I made my excuses and withdrew.

Chapter 10

The Expansion Benefit Decision. The Anti-Withdrawal System in Consultancy Practice

Later, in the restaurant where I was eating a dinner which would have cost me a week's salary, had I been earning a salary, my attention was drawn to two Englishmen dining at a nearby table. One was a large, heavily built man eating with so much enjoyment that it was obvious he had not looked at the prices, and his companion was a dapper little chap whose anxious expression indicated that he had. The big man shouted to me in a high pitched voice, 'Don't touch the strawberries', and I smiled back and said that I did not intend to.

'Here on business?' the big man shouted, and I nodded, wondering why he had sorted me out, and hoping that the conversation was now at an end. I have never enjoyed talking to strange men, and this one looked as though he had more than a passing interest in the white slave trade. I was quite wrong, however, because when I met him again in the bar he confided that he and his friend were in the hair business.

'What is the hair business?' I asked. 'Are you hairdressers?'

'Oh, no', said the large one, who introduced himself as Arnold Peaman and his friend as Mervyn Flank. 'We have hair clinics all over Europe. You must have heard of us, Mervarn Hair Clinics, we advertise everywhere.'

'We also have a wig business', said Mervyn. 'Here, this is us', he said, handing me a Dutch magazine with a half-page advertisement headed 'True-Top'. I could understand very little of it, but it had two photographs side by side, one of an evil looking bald man scowling and the other of the same man, hairy and smiling. There was a coupon at the bottom of the advertisement for bald Dutchmen to complete and send to an Amsterdam address.

'Very impressive', I said. 'How do you reconcile your hair clinics, which presumably claim to grow hair, with your wig business, which virtually admits defeat and offers a substitute?'

'A good question', said Arnold. 'He asks a good question, doesn't he Merv?'

'He certainly does', agreed Mervyn. 'The answer is, we keep both businesses entirely separate. No one is aware that we own both Mervarn and True-Top. By the way, what business are you in?'

'I am a Management Consultant', I said.

'I'm not surprised', said Arnold. 'I thought you were a shrewd boy, as soon as I saw you, didn't I, Merv?'

Mervyn agreed. 'Canny', he said. 'We are used to summing up characters quickly. We do it all day.'

Arnold said, 'Where is your practice?'

'Here', I said airily. 'Holland, Germany, all Western Europe.'

They exchanged a glance. 'What type of business do you specialise in?' Arnold asked.

'Education, chiefly', I said. 'I am at present hired by Atomic Reading, to supervise its management structure and to open institutes throughout the continent.' I then had to explain what Atomic Reading was, and they were both very interested.

'It is a similar business to the hair business', Arnold said.

'Surely not', I protested, pointing out that Atomic Reading was a high-minded endeavour to reorganise the world's educational system, while the hair business was purely of cosmetic interest.

Arnold smiled tolerantly. 'It is similar in so far as we both attract customers through advertising, and then immediately have to extract substantial sums of money from them.'

'That, in its crudest form, is a description of every business which advertises', I said.

'True, true', said Mervyn, ordering me yet another cognac at six guilders. 'How long have you been operating in Holland?'

I looked at my watch, through a haze. 'Almost exactly ten hours', I said.

'So you have a pretty good idea of the business situation here in the Netherlands?' Arnold said.

'Oh, yes', I agreed. 'I've seen quite a bit.'

I found it necessary, at that moment, to pay a short visit to the *Herren*, and when I returned my two drinking companions looked at me for a few seconds without speaking. Then Mervyn said, 'We have a proposition for you. Hear me well.'

I have always been a sucker for propositions, so I sat back, cigar in one hand and cognac in the other, and composed my features to fit in with the situation—forehead slightly wrinkled, eyes hooded but alert, lower lip fractionally protruding, with just a hint of amused cynicism playing around the mouth. I learnt it from the old television serial, 'The Power Game', and I had been waiting for several years for the chance to use it.

'Arnold and I', said little Mervyn, 'would like to know whether you are interested in taking on another client. We have considerable business interests in Holland, as well as Belgium, Germany, France, Italy . . . have I left anywhere out, Arn?'

106

'Spain, Switzerland. . . .' Arnold said. 'I think that's it, Merv. Apart, of course, from Great Britain.'

'We have been travelling all over Europe for several years,' Mervyn continued, 'because we run our companies personally. We started them, and apart from an administrative office in each country usually run by a local accountant, we control them ourselves. We have never employed anyone to whom we could delegate overall management, because firstly, we quite enjoy travelling—we are both married, you see—and secondly, because we have never trusted anyone.'

Arnold then took up the story. 'We have considered employing an assistant, but it is not easy to find someone with the necessary management ability who would be prepared to live on the continent permanently. Our conversation with you this evening has been very interesting. You obviously have the management experience, and your ten years in Holland prove that. . . .'

I did not hear any more. They thought that I had said ten years in Holland. Should I enlighten them? Somebody once said—well, I forget what they said, but the gist was that opportunities do not occur very often, and when they do they should be grasped firmly with both hands. Besides, they might leave me to pay for the drinks.

'I am sure that I could handle another client', I said. 'Tell me about your businesses.'

'The Mervarn Hair Clinics', said Arnold, 'deal primarily with people who have hair and scalp problems. Each clinic is fully staffed with a manager, who is an experienced trichologist, an assistant manager and a team of female operators. They make us a great deal of money, but they are prone to periodic spells of bad publicity. The media have no sense of honour when it comes to hair clinics. They are content to accept vast advertising revenue from us, yet they will attack us whenever they are short of a few columns of copy. We are an easy target. We are aware that we can be closed down at any time. One error in our advertisement, one claim that we can grow hair on the head of a bald man, and we have broken the law.'

'If you cannot claim to grow hair, what is your reason for existence?' I asked.

'We claim to cure scalp disorders', Mervyn said. 'We can keep hair healthy. We can help to reduce hair loss. A man who, in the normal course of events, will be bald in two years, can delay the process almost indefinitely by receiving treatment at a Mervarn clinic. We have a loyal clientele, and a dedicated staff.'

'In that case,' I said, 'what do you require from me?'

'Keep us safe from detrimental publicity,' Arnold said, 'and stop our dedicated managers from thieving.'

'Your other business, gentlemen. Will you please give me details?'

'This is comparatively simple', Mervyn said. 'Knowing that our hair clinics are based on sand, and that one over-zealous Member of Parliament probing too deeply can put us out of business, we had to find an alternative: one that would complement the clinics, yet be entirely separate. Consequently, we decided to cash in on the wig game—wigs for men, that is, not women. In America and England it is already a big thing. Here on the continent it is in its infancy, and we are the first real operators.'

'This sounds interesting,' I said, 'but once again, how can I help?'

'We need growth and organisation,' Arnold said, 'ideas and energy: recruitment and training of salesmen.'

'And a foolproof method', said Mervyn, 'to stop our salesmen thieving.'

'Are continentals particularly prone to thieving?' I asked.

'Oh, yes', said Arnold. 'In six years of travelling the length and breadth of Europe, we have found the common denominator which unites the European community of nations. We would put it down to their natural resentment at being employed by Englishmen, but for the fact that our English companies are as adept at the game as any. In fact, it is a source of national pride to me and Merv that our Newcastle branch devised the cleverest method yet of cooking the books.'

'On the other hand,' said Mervyn, 'the bigger the crook, the better the salesman. We know that De Vries, our manager in The Hague, is robbing us blind, but his figures are so good that we let him get away with it. If we fired him it would cost us ten thousand guilders a month.'

'There is one point that we have not yet discussed', I said. 'It is the small matter of my remuneration.'

'That is indeed a small matter,' said Arnold, 'which Mervyn and I will talk about later. Rest assured that it will be substantial. Meanwhile, we can offer you a luxurious apartment in Kalvestraat, the Bond Street of Amsterdam. We have a True-Top wig shop there, and the top floor has been converted into a flat. Where do you usually stay in Amsterdam?'

'At the moment,' I said, 'I am staying here, at the Hilton.'

'There you are', Arnold said triumphantly. 'At twelve pounds a day, you will be saving eighty-four pounds a week. That's not bad for a start, is it? You can move in tomorrow.'

I was too tired to work it out, but it did seem that my accommodation problem had been solved. I now had three companies and an apartment. All I needed to be a really successful Management Consultant was someone to pay me some money.

I could not decide whether to tell Bob Bishop that I had been hired by Mervarn Hair Clinics and True-Top (Nederland) NV. As a freelance I was entitled to take on as many clients as I could handle, and I was certain that Atomic Reading would not suffer because of my extra interests. As it happened, the question did not arise, because Bob was in such a state of advanced exhaustion when I called at his room in the morning that he could not talk coherently. All he said was, 'Carry me to the airport.' In the taxi he collapsed again, and I did not get another word out of him until I left him at the check-in. There he took my hand, more as a means of keeping on his feet than a farewell, and said ambiguously, 'Keep it warm for me, kiddo.'

'I will', I promised, and he staggered out of sight.

It was a busy day. I returned to the Hilton and collected my case, and went directly to the True-Top shop in Kalvestraat. A slim man in a navy-blue suit advanced as I opened the door, and before I could open my mouth he had pushed me to a chair. He looked closely at my hair and shook his head sadly. He started a torrent of Dutch, but I interrupted him and said, 'I am English.'

'I could tell at once', he lied. 'I can always tell an Englishman. They clean their shoes every day. But your wig is not good. I can see the lining.'

'I am not wearing a wig', I said.

This stopped him only momentarily. 'Have you got any English cigarettes?' he said. I handed him a packet, and he took three and placed them carefully in his own pack of Benson and Hedges.

'You've got your own English cigarettes', I protested.

'Yes,' he said, 'but they are very expensive here.'

'Are you the manager of this shop?' I asked him.

'Yes', he said. 'It is the best wig shop in Holland, and I am the best wig salesman in Holland.'

'It sounds like an unbeatable combination', I said.

'You know what I sell here?' he asked me, and then used a familiar expression indicating that he sold nothing at all.

'You speak English very well', I told him. 'Where did you pick up that particular phrase?'

'I lived in Australia for eight years', he said. 'I'm an Aussie, you Pommy bastard.'

'Why do you sell nothing?' I said.

'In Milano', he said, 'True-Top has an office on the tenth floor of a big building in a back street. There we sell sixty wigs a month. In Paris our office is on the second floor above a bank, and we sell over a hundred wigs a month. In Utrecht we have a dirty little upstairs room, two kilometres from the centre of the city, where we sell thirty a month. Here, in the main street, with a beautiful shop, with photographs in the window, we are lucky to sell ten wigs a month. Why? Because men will not come into a shop where everyone can see them buying a wig. If a man wants to buy a wig, he does it in his own home when the salesman calls, or in some little street where he can slip in secretly. This is a big mistake, this shop.'

The door opened and in, like a modern Sydney Greenstreet and Peter Lorre, came big Mr Peaman and little Mr Flank. They both wore overcoats with velvet collars, and each carried a briefcase. They looked indescribably sinister.

'Ah!' said Arnold Peaman. 'You have met Albert. Our best salesman, Mr B.'

'So he was telling me', I said.

'Albert Konig', said Mervyn Flank, 'earns more than the Prime Minister of Holland.'

'He also', said Albert, 'owes more, and his wife, she spends more.'

Arnold said, 'Mr Bennett is a Management Consultant, and he will be advising us on methods to improve the efficiency of our interests here. You will regard him, Albert, as the overall manager of True-Top, and you will work very closely with him. In fact, he will be living in the flat upstairs, so he will always be on hand if you have any problem you wish to discuss.'

Albert looked furious. 'I have been sleeping upstairs', he said. 'I have all my clothes there.'

'Well, move them out, Albert. Go home to your wife', said Mervyn.

They took me upstairs to the top floor, and I looked around at my new home. It was not luxurious, but it was clean and comfortable.

'Have you had a chance to consider my earnings?' I asked.

'Not yet, old boy', Arnold said. 'You just settle yourself in here first, and we'll talk about it later. By the way, watch Albert carefully, don't trust him an inch. We think that he makes sales here in the shop, and then supplies the wig personally and pockets the cash. Try and set a trap for him.'

'I am a Management Consultant,' I said with dignity, 'not a private detective.'

'Management Consultants', said Mervyn, 'are the private detectives of the business world.'

'How interesting', I said. 'Strange that I have never heard it before.'

'Not really', said Arnold. 'Merv just made it up.'

'Will you explain the wig business to me?' I asked them.

110

'Sure', Arnold said. We sat down in my sitting-room, and he began. 'Our business is based on the effectiveness of our advertising. Here in Holland we spend about ten thousand guilders a month— that is over a thousand pounds. We use magazines and national newspapers mostly. Each country is different. In Britain we concentrate on the Sunday papers, but there are no Sunday papers in Holland.'

'Do you use the popular or the quality papers to advertise in?' I asked.

'The popular ones every time. Advertising agencies will always try to persuade you to use the better-class media, but it is a waste of money. This is strictly a working and lower-middle class business. We get the occasional lawyer or executive as a client, but the vast majority of wig purchasers are ordinary working men.'

'I suppose the prospective client completes the coupon and returns it to you. What happens then?'

'We send him a brochure and a letter, and two or three days later one of our salesmen calls at his home in the evening to try and make a sale.'

'How much are the wigs?'

'They vary from, in English money, a hundred pounds to a hundred and eighty.'

'What is the difference between a hundred pound wig and one for a hundred and eighty pounds?'

'Eighty pounds', said Mervyn, who was establishing himself as a wit.

'No, seriously', I said.

'That is serious', said Arnold. 'There is no actual difference. The salesman just gets the best price he can. It makes a big difference in commission. We pay ten pounds commission for a hundred pound wig, and thirty pounds for a hundred and eighty pound sale.'

'And how much does the wig cost you?'

'This varies,' Arnold said, 'depending on the length and colour of the hair. A basic wig costs us fifteen pounds.'

I was silent, but only for a moment. 'I think I have the hang of the wig business', I said.

Job Encouragement and Summit Counsel Procedure for Mid-Stratum Management

Arnold and Mervyn had some personal business to talk over with Albert, so I took a taxi to the Atomic Reading Institute. I arrived just in time for the twelve-thirty demonstration. There was one person in the audience. Mr Klein gave him the full treatment, but at the end of his hour-long speech the audience stood up and left without a word.

'Not very successful, Mr Klein', I said.

'No,' he agreed, 'but it could be worse.'

'How could it possibly be worse?' I said.

'Suppose', he said, giving me an invaluable glimpse of the sheer logic of the Dutch, 'that there had been ten people at the demonstration, and all ten had walked out. Then we would have lost ten clients, and that would have been terrible. Today, we lost only one client.'

'If we didn't hold any demonstrations at all', I said, 'we wouldn't lose any clients, and look at the money we would save on advertising.'

Mr Klein considered this statement, sucking at his pipe with great thought, trying to find the flaw in the theory. Apparently unable to do so, he said, 'Is this to be your first action, to cancel the advertising?'

'No', I said. 'Increase it, but not by paying for it. We must obtain greater publicity. I shall suggest to Mr Bishop that we engage a public relations man who will arrange a press conference. Meanwhile, get me details of your most successful student, your oldest and youngest students, and your prettiest girl student. Have a talk with our advertising agency and get their ideas. I shall have another discussion with you tomorrow.'

'Are you not returning for tonight's demonstrations?' he said. 'Your reading skill is invaluable to us.'

'You will have to manage without me', I said. 'I have retired from active demonstrations. I have, as it were, hung up my, er, eyes.'

Satisfied that I had created some positive thinking, I returned to the True-Top shop, where I was just in time to join Arnold and Mervyn for their inspection of the Amsterdam Mervarn Hair Clinic. This was a mile from the city centre, in a pleasant thoroughfare which combined bourgeois respectability with solid prosperity. The clinic was a double-fronted shop with a tasteful fascia and a window display of photographic blow-ups. Consultations, said a small notice, were gratis.

We entered the shop, greeted by an aroma of mild disinfectant, and a hospital hush. The receptionist, white-coated, was painting her fingernails.

'Hello, my little sweetheart', said Arnold, placing his arm paternally around her shoulders. 'How much money is in the till?'

'About four hundred and fifty guilders, Mr Peaman', she said.

'Give me four hundred', said Arnold. 'Make out a chit for travel expenses. I'll sign it.' He took the money, gave half to Mervyn, and said, 'Make us some coffee, love. We'll be in the office. Oh, and bring in the daily report sheets for the month.'

I followed them to the rear of the shop, passing two rows of cubicles, each containing a comfortable chair facing a looking-glass.

112

Three of the cubicles were occupied by clients, and each client was being treated by a micro-skirted girl standing behind him. The treatment seemed to consist of a vague poking at the scalp with a little wooden stick, but what impressed me more was the way these young ladies were thrusting their ample Dutch bosoms into their patients' ears. I wondered whether this was a new method of treating itching scalp, because if so I felt that the Mervarn Hair Clinics were on to something good. I asked Mervyn to explain, and he did. 'These poor buggers pay twenty guilders per treatment', he said. 'They deserve something more than a slap on the bonce with a bit of cotton wool soaked in Dettol.'

The manager's office looked like a doctor's surgery. Charts on the walls illustrated what disasters could occur to a man's follicles unless he took the correct precautions, and I immediately started to scratch.

'Hans,' said Arnold to the manager, who stiffened with fear as we entered, 'how much have you taken this month?'

'It has not been easy', said Hans. 'The advertisements have not been pulling, Mr Peaman. I have only one consultation booked today.'

'We'll go through the reports together', said Arnold. 'This is Mr Gordon Bennett, Hans. He is a Management Consultant who specialises in the hair business, and he has been engaged by the company to direct and rejuvenate us all.

Hans said, 'Pleased to meet you sir, I am Gerard Pranger.'

'Why do you call him Hans', I asked Mervyn, 'when his name is Gerard?'

'Because he is always interfering with his girl operators', Mervyn explained.

Together we sat around the desk and examined the complicated daily report forms. 'On the first of the month you had 6 consultations', read Arnold. 'Only 1 was enrolled for a course of 25 treatments. All the others were missed. Hopeless, Hans, terrible!' Arnold was frightening in his anger, and poor Hans cringed. Mervyn turned the page. 'The next day was better', he said. 'You took 3,600 guilders. Very good, Hans. Two enrolments, and 3 re-enrolments. And you sold some home treatment kits for 500 guilders each. Terrific, Hans.' Hans smiled.

Arnold took over for the third of the month. 'What a lousy day. You missed everything. And you let Mr Wanmakers finish his treatments. Why didn't you re-enroll him?'

'Please, Mr Peaman,' Hans said, 'he had 150 treatments here. He was such a good customer, I re-enrolled him 6 times.'

'Why didn't you re-enroll him for the seventh time?' Arnold barked.

H   113

Hans almost wept. 'He had no hair left, Mr Peaman.'

'So what's wrong with scalp massage?' Arnold asked.

We went through the rest of the month. It was the twenty-seventh, and the clinic had taken 30,000 guilders. To me it seemed good business, but Arnold was not happy. 'The Hague has taken 45,000, Rotterdam nearly 40,000. Even Utrecht has taken 25,000. It's not good enough, Hans. 'Forty-five thousand next month, and you will earn yourself a big bonus. Otherwise, out.'

Leaving Hans to deal with a new client, we went out to reception.

'Hans is cracking up', Mervyn said, 'The pressure is too great, having to sell and resell the same idea day after day, never a let-up, always having to beat last month's figures. Only the nut-cases last, the sadists and the megalomaniacs who glory in the power they can wield over their clients.'

'What power?' I asked. 'After all, it's only hair.'

'*Only* hair!' said Mervyn. 'You have a lot to learn about this business, laddie. The fear of going bald is so intense in some men that every hair on their comb is like a finger dropping off. When such a man sees his hair line receding he will spend every penny he has for a cure, but there isn't one. He will come to us, God willing, and we will wash his hair, powder it, shine lights on it and spread fertiliser on it. A top manager, like the one we have in London, will have him standing on his head singing "Land of Hope and Glory", but managers like that are hard to find. Hans is too soft. I give him another month or two, and then we shall have to replace him. It will be up to you to find us a new manager.'

'But I know nothing about trichology', I said.

'Neither do our managers', Mervyn said. 'Just find us a salesman. Two weeks instruction at our London clinic and he'll learn all he'll ever need to know.'

'I am not sure', I said thoughtfully, 'whether the Institute of Management Consultants would approve of this business.'

'Why not?' Mervyn said. 'We are perfectly legal. Our advertising agencies approve, so do the newspapers and magazines which print our ads. The banks approve, we give them a lot of business. We employ many people at above-average salaries. To our clients we supply hope, an invaluable commodity. We cannot cure baldness, but we can end dandruff.'

'So can a bottle of good shampoo', I said.

'Look,' said Mervyn, 'we are not asking you to do anything unethical. We do not expect you to sell hair treatments. Just keep our business running economically, smooth over any problems which may occur, keep a careful eye on the cash, and never, never refund a client's money.'

114

'That reminds me', I said. 'I must reach a financial agreement with you.'

'Later', he said. 'What's the matter with you? Don't you trust us?'

Professionalism in the Head-to-Head Encounter. Direct Marketing to Domestic Consumers of Semi-Durables

True-Top (Nederland) NV.—'hair-pieces for the discerning man'— was doing well. Although business in the True-Top shop continued to be poor, our advertisements were bringing in more coupons than ever, and Albert was making a fortune in commission. His confidence was high, and his rate of converting enquiries to sales reached the record level of two to one.

'How do you do it, Albert?' I asked him in admiration, when he called at my flat one evening having sold three wigs in three hours, and making himself seventy-five pounds.

'Because I am a professional salesman', he said. 'Your other salesmen, they are part-time, and if they make a sale it is useful drinking money, and if they miss it they still eat. Me, I have to sell or I don't eat. You need other salesmen like me, except that there is no one else like me in Holland. Come out with me tomorrow night, and I show you how a professional salesman sells a wig.'

The next evening Albert and I set out armed with six coupons. Our first call was a meneer Kegels, who lived in East Amsterdam, an old part of town quite un-Dutch-like in its shabby untidiness. Albert knocked at the door, and it was opened by a bald man in his shirt sleeves. He carried a newspaper in his hand, and his braces were dangling; he was the international symbol of the man who had just come out of the lavatory. Albert walked inside, neatly sidestepping meneer Kegels. I stayed on the doorstep. Kegels said something to me, which I naturally failed to grasp, and then he turned and broke into a trot, trying to catch up with Albert who was proceeding along the passage to the living-room. I heard the raised voice of meneer Kegels, then the raised voice of mevrouw Kegels, and then the raised voice of Albert. Then I heard the giggling of children, and then the very raised voice of meneer Kegels. Then I heard the sound of a sharp blow, followed by a wail. 'My God', I thought. 'Albert is being attacked', and I was in two minds whether to stay where I was or run for the car, but Albert and Kegels appeared again, exchanging sharp epithets, and the slamming of the front door ended my first encounter with a True-Top potential client.

'A hoax', said Albert bitterly. 'His bloody kids sent in the coupon for a joke.'

'Do you get many hoaxes?' I said.

'About one in ten coupons is a hoax', Albert said. 'Never mind, we're off to Amstelveen.'

As we stopped outside the neat little house in the fashionable suburb of Amstelveen, Albert adjusted his own wig with care, combing a few careless strands down over his forehead and defining the parting carefully. Then, grasping his black bag, he strode up to the front door with me a few steps behind him. A woman answered his knock. 'Meneer Vink,' said Albert, once again easing his way into the house before the woman could stop him, 'I have an appointment with meneer Vink. True-Top.'

We were taken into a Dutch living-room, clean and somewhat Victorian, with plants growing everywhere. A middle-aged man wearing spectacles looked up from the television with surprise. His two flaxen horse-faced daughters looked up with interest.

'I'm from True-Top, meneer', Albert said, sitting down at the table and pulling out a chair for me. 'Come and sit here, meneer.' In a daze meneer Vink joined us. His wife and daughters stood behind him. Meneer Vink grinned in embarrassment and said, 'Meneer, I did not expect you. I only sent a coupon for interest, I do not really want a wig.' He looked around at his family and shrugged, and it was obvious that he had not informed them of his interest. Albert ignored his protests, and opened his black bag. He took out his red presentation book, his roll of plastic, his scissors and sticky tape dispenser, and arranged them before him neatly. He began to speak quietly, turning the pages of his book and showing the photographs of men with bald heads on the left, and the same men wearing hair-pieces on the right. The Vink family were impressed. Heavy Dutch witticisms passed between the girls and their father, with whistles of amazement at the transformations. Meneer Vink touched his bald head lightly and looked at his wife appealingly. She just said, 'How much?' Albert, seeing where the power lay, began to work on mevrouw Vink.

'Your husband, mevrouw, will look a young man again, and he will feel a young man.' Mevrouw Vink tightened her lips, not pleased at the prospect of a rejuvenated meneer Vink, and Albert immediately picked up her mood and changed the subject slightly.

'He will become more confident and will take you out more', he said, 'instead of staying at home every night to watch television. He will want to buy you new clothes, so that you also will feel youthful and look beautiful like him.'

'I don't want new clothes', mevrouw Vink said. 'I want a new washing machine', but she was definitely softening.

Albert went into his closing speech, telling them about the high quality of a True-Top wig. 'Every hair put in by hand and double

116

knotted. A genuine silk parting, wherever you want it. The finest north European hair, not coarse Turkish or Greek. You know what the other firms use? Chinese hair! Do you want your husband, after twenty years of married life, to wear Chinese hair?'

'No!' shuddered the wife and the daughters.

'And the price for a superb, best quality wig for your husband, that will last nearly for ever? Made in England, near the place where Churchill lived? The price is fourteen hundred guilders', and Albert's hands shot up to his head and whipped off his own wig.

The effect was truly startling. The good-looking thirty-year-old Albert suddenly became the ugly forty-year-old Albert—head as bald as an egg. The daughters clutched each other, and mevrouw Vink gripped her husband's shoulder. It was as much of a shock to me as it had been to them, because I hadn't understood a word of the conversation. I thought he had gone berserk.

Albert put back his wig, and unhurriedly took from his bag an order pad. He unrolled his plastic sheeting and placed it over meneer Vink's head, fixing it with sticky tape into an accurate mould of his scalp. He marked the position of the parting, cut off a small piece of Vink's remaining hair as a colour sample, and then completed the order form and contract.

'I need a four hundred guilder deposit', he said. 'I can accept cash or a giro.'

Mr Vink took from his wallet four hundred guilder notes, and Albert wrote a receipt. 'In three weeks you must come to our place in Amsterdam for a first fitting', he said. 'Bring mevrouw with you if you like, and your lovely daughters.' He slid all his paraphernalia into his black bag, shook hands with the Vinks and was gone, leaving me still sitting with them. They all stared at me, wondering perhaps if I was to be left there as some kind of surety. I stood up, flushing, and shook hands silently. Then I made a little dignified bow, which meneer Vink reciprocated, and raced out to the car. Albert shot off like a bank robber towards our next client at Noordwijk, repeating word for word the conversation he had had with the Vinks.

'Once you get the money in your hand,' he said, 'you go quickly before they change their mind.'

'I'll remember in future', I said.

Noordwijk was bleak, as are most of the towns on the North Sea coast, and Albert had to hold his wig on firmly as we stepped out of the car into a cold, wet gale. Potential customer Smeerdijk lived in one of those blocks of flats which are the bane of salesmen, because after ringing the bell, one has to announce oneself through a speaking tube.

'Meneer Smeerdijk,' said Albert, 'this is Konig, the barber from True-Top.'

'I don't want to see you', said the invisible Smeerdijk.

'You must', said Albert. 'I've come from Amsterdam.'

'Nobody asked you to', said Smeerdijk. 'You'd better go back.'

'But I've brought the English director of the company with me,' Albert said, 'all the way from Stoke-on-Trent.' I understood enough Dutch by this time to recognise the fact that I was being brought into the affair, and I started to walk away. Albert grabbed my coat.

'Let me speak to the Englishman', said Smeerdijk.

'How do you do, sir', I said into the grille. 'It is a pleasure to make your acquaintance.'

'How do you do', said Smeerdijk in English. 'It is also a pleasure to speak to you, and if you do not go away at once I shall phone the foreign police and have you exported from the country.'

'Goodbye, meneer Smeerdijk', I said.

'Goodbye, mister', said Smeerdijk.

'May you stay bald for the rest of your life', shouted Albert, white with rage.

We drove in silence to Leiden, where I refused to get out of the car, so Albert went in alone and emerged half an hour later with a contract for a 999 guilder wig. Then we went to a little village called Uithoorn, where, when we finally located the address, we were driven away with curses because it was nearly midnight.

At half-past one in the morning, in an Amsterdam bar, Albert created a mild sensation by removing his wig and placing it on the counter, over my glass of cognac. I was mortified, but the barman, a huge man with three strands of hair carefully arranged across a naked pate, was both entertained and interested, and Albert made an appointment for the following day.

'You make a lot of money, Albert,' I said, as he drove me home at three o'clock, 'but you earn every guilder.'

'You're right,' he agreed, 'particularly as I am not really bald. I shave my head every morning.'

'You're crazy', I said.

'No I'm not', he said. 'I'm a professional salesman.'

Principles of Labour Rotation in the Heteromorphic Marketing Environment

I soon became accustomed to constant travel. One day I was at True-Top in Paris, the next day at the Mervarn Hair Clinic in Zurich, then on to True-Top Milan and Rome, and back to Amsterdam via Brussels, Rotterdam and The Hague. I checked the books at each establishment, examined the response to advertisements, rejected requests for salary increases, refused refunds to customers, and wrote reports to London. My three companies fitted well together, and I experienced little difficulty in dealing successively with cases of falling hair at the clinics, fading wigs at True-Top, and failing eyesights at Atomic Reading institutes.

I opened three new Atomic schools at Rotterdam, The Hague and Groningen, and I was particularly successful in utilising the rotation of labour principle. The head of the Rotterdam school was the former manager of the Mervarn Hair Clinic in Utrecht, and my chief instructor at The Hague Atomic Reading Institute was a failed wig salesman from Haarlem.

Not all my experiments in switching staff came off. When Mr Klein, the principal of Amsterdam Atomic Reading, took his vacation, I had to find someone to take the next series of demonstrations, and I persuaded Albert to try. I coached him carefully, until he knew the whole wonderful story as well as I, and he made his debut before an unusually large audience. His eyes glinted when he saw so many bald heads together, but I forbade him to solicit any new wig business.

Albert was a total failure at Atomic Reading. Not being able to speak or understand Dutch, I was unaware that Albert spoke an appalling version of his mother tongue, ungrammatical and colloquial, with an Amsterdam accent so pronounced as to render him almost incomprehensible to our intellectual gathering. The Dutch are very conscious of the quality of speech, far more so than the British, and from the moment he opened his mouth our cause was lost. I was ignorant of this until told by a horrified instructor, but in any event we would have had no acceptances that evening. Albert, obviously rattled by the lack of response from his audience, hurried towards the soft sell close.

'The cost of our Atomic Reading course, ladies and gentlemen, is 550 guilders', he said, and raising his hands to his head, he whipped off his wig.

Resource Allocation and the Variable Transport Factor

The Cologne branch of Atomisches Lesen (Deutschland) GmbH was almost ready to open for business. I had interviewed at least fifty Germans, and had selected a principal and a staff of twelve part-timers, and had them fully trained to read and teach speed reading the Atomic way. The advertising agency had devised some new advertisements, and space had been booked in the two local newspapers. I had opened a bank account, although no money had yet been deposited. All that remained to be done was to finalise the formation of the company, and this required a visit to a notary with the directors. I telephoned Bob Bishop, and he arranged to fly to Cologne with the company accountant, a nice young man named Patrick Coogan. I met them at the airport, and we made our way to the lawyer's office. Herr Filbinger greeted us with grave news: the Rhine had flooded, and the notary had been unable to leave his home. We would have to postpone our business until tomorrow.

'Impossible', said Bob. 'I'm a busy man, Herr Fillibuster, and I cannot afford to waste a day. If the notary cannot come to us, we shall go to him.'

A taxi took us to a village a few miles south of Cologne, but we could not get within two hundred yards of the notary's house, which was in an avenue leading down to the river. The entire road was flooded to a depth of three feet, and we stood staring impotently at our destination. Some children were happily floating on a plank, and one was sitting in a large drawer. Another boy was on a red rubber seal, and paddled towards us. Herr Filbinger gave him a mark, and asked him to deliver a message to the notary. He splashed away.

'Good luck, son', said Bob, between clenched teeth. 'May God go with you.' He came to attention and held a salute. Herr Filbinger was visibly affected.

The message was delivered, and the notary appeared at an upstairs window and waved. We waved back. A few minutes later four men in blue boiler suits began to wade towards us, through water which reached their hips. Their leader spoke to Herr Filbinger, who then addressed us.

'Schentlemen, these four common vorkmen, plumbers I think, who are engaged in poomping out the vater from the notary's basement, vill carry us across the floodings.'

We could not believe it. 'Not plumbers', said Patrick. 'It's impossible. My plumber at home won't even answer the phone.'

The workmen, all grizzled men in their fifties, looked at Bob with anxiety. He was a heavily built man, and he also looked anxious. Herr Filbinger did not hesitate. Nimbly he leapt on the back of his chosen mount, tucked his coat tails in, and leaned forward in a truly professional manner as though he had been riding plumbers all his life. I climbed diffidently upon my plumber and Patrick, with extreme care, mounted his, a smallish man who suspended Patrick's bottom a mere four inches above water level. With a great deal of grunting from both Bob and his mount, we were finally all aboard, and we began our perilous journey.

'Let's have a race', suggested Bob, his confidence restored by the

120

obvious sea-worthiness of his plumber. 'Last one at the notary is a stinking fink.'

I was genuinely touched by the kindly gesture of these honest workmen, and although we had not been introduced, I felt that it was up to me to make some polite conversation. 'It's quite a nice day, isn't it?' I said.

'Bitte?' said my mount.

'Apart from the flood', I said. There was no response. I tried again. 'My first trip on the Rhine, actually', I said. He grunted.

'*Sprecken zie Deutsch?*' I asked.

'*Ja*', he said.

'Oh, of course you do', I said. 'Sorry, I mean *sprecken zie Englische?*'

'*Nein*', he said. This ended my attempts at conversation.

Herr Filbinger was not talking but concentrating on keeping his mount on a straight course. Patrick was too concerned about keeping his bottom, which kept slipping lower, out of the Rhine. Bob was chattering to his man non-stop, trying to enrol him on an Atomic Reading course, and promising him a substantial reduction if he would agree to become personal plumber, by appointment, to Atomisches Lesen (Deutschland) GmbH.

I was the first to dismount at the notary's house, beating Herr Filbinger by a short head. Bob was a long way behind.

'Next trip I want your plumber', he said when he finally arrived. 'This one is over the top. His wind has broken.' His mount looked rather as though his back was broken.

The ceremony with the notary was over quite quickly, and after a glass of sherry and handshakes all round, we started back. There was a minor mutiny amongst the plumbers, none of whom wanted to carry Bob, and for a while it seemed that he would have to return on the red seal, but German discipline prevailed after some shouting by the notary and Filbinger.

'Hey, Herr Fillibuster', said Bob suddenly, in mid-stream. 'I'd like to try a little social experiment. Tell them they're carrying four Polish Jews on their backs across the Rhine.'

Filbinger was not amused, and I said irritably, 'Shut up, Bob. Do you want to start the whole thing all over again?'

Chapter 11

A Short Study of the European Economic Community Nationally Evaluated

Loss of national identity, it was claimed by many, would be one of the fearsome results of Great Britain's membership of the Common Market. Only time will tell, but if it is any comfort to our nationalists, my travels in Western Europe failed to disclose any signs of it among the six original countries. It is wrong to generalise in a scholarly treatise of this nature, but let me state clearly and definitely that nobody loves the Germans. Nobody, in fact, even likes the Germans, and as for identifying with them nationally, most Europeans would prefer the unknown inhabitants of Venus. This does not prevent their partners in the Economic Community respecting them and buying their cars by the million. There is universal admiration for German achievements, workers, money, and beer, but Germany remains secure within her borders.

Nobody loves the French, except the French. They are isolated by their language, which their partners agree is a beautiful language, but not for them. They are considered greedy, selfish and rude, but they are respected for their cognac, their perfume, and their cars. And their food, of course. There is also a sneaking regard for the prices of their hotels, particularly in Paris, and visitors vie with each other, like anglers with their fishing stories, over the amount of their bills.

Nobody loves the Belgians, not even the Belgians. The Dutch laugh at them, the rest of the Community ignore them. The antipathy between the French-speaking Walloons and the Flemings is so great that I had to open a True-Top office in Antwerp because the Flemish speakers would not deal with my French-speaking manager in Brussels.

I once saw a shop assistant in Antwerp refuse to serve a Walloon, and this was the only occasion in my experience of the Common Market when the Great Equaliser, Money, failed to speak the language of conciliation.

The Italians are not hated, but they are looked upon as second-class members of the Community by the North Europeans. This does not worry the irrepressible Italians, who are the great travellers in Europe. They appear everywhere, as workers and café owners, and even if they are occasionally banned from Amsterdam bars and discos, they seem popular with northern girls. Despised as they may be, they are respected for their men's fashions and their cars.

The Dutch are disliked by the Belgians, who consider them mean and untrustworthy. They are treated tolerantly by the Germans, who regard them as misguided and less efficient members of their own people, a point of view not shared by Dutchmen. The French despise their cheese, and the Italians their climate. Dutch Catholics and Dutch Protestants do not like each other, but they are too civilised to fight about it.

I met no one who disliked Luxembourgers, and I met no one who liked them. I met no one, in fact, who had ever seen a Luxembourger, but I believe that they do exist, living lives of affluence and peace, with an unemployed population which occasionally reaches double figures, and with no desire whatsoever to lose their national identity.

As a Briton, what did I think of the Common Market inhabitants? I loved them all, with the possible exception of the stone-throwing student international, who are very, very hard to love.

But I was always glad to go home.

Psychological Advertising Related to Hidden Activity Forecasting and Nominal Regression Analysis

I was always particularly glad to go home when somebody else paid the fare, and when Arnold Peaman sent me a return KLM ticket, with a request for my attendance at a meeting in London, I knew that it must be important because Arnold did not throw his money about needlessly. The meeting was held at his Mayfair headquarters, and the managers of all the European True-Top businesses were present.

'Mervyn and I have just returned from the United States,' said Arnold, 'and we have brought back the greatest innovation in the hair business. Hair weaving, it is called, and it will make a lot of money for all of you.'

'And you too, we hope, Mr Peaman', said Signor Baroni from Milan, an irreverent man, later to prove to be a dastardly double-agent who set up his own business, Signor-Top, in Italy.

'We hope to make a crust', Arnold said agreeably. 'Hair weaving is a method of attaching hair to the head permanently, without a transplant or a toupee. It is a marvel of modern science, and it will transform the wig business. Mervyn will now explain the technicalities.'

Mervyn Flank stood up and glanced around the room. 'Make sure that door is shut', he said to me quietly. 'We cannot be too careful.

Now, gentlemen, hear me well. First of all, a hair weave can only be made on a man who still has some hair on his head. It is useless for the completely bald man. Now, look at this.' He held up a circular object, about six inches in diameter, like the strings of a tennis racquet. 'This is a hair weave base, and these criss-cross strands are made of nylon. The base is tied to the client's scalp by his own hair. It is knotted very tightly, so that it is immovable. Then, hair is woven on to this framework, and the subject has a fine, permanent head of hair which he can wash, brush and even restyle.'

We were all delighted by this fantastic invention which, if it really worked, would give us a tremendous lead over our competitors.

'The system has been used in the States for a long time,' Arnold said. 'chiefly on negroes, when it was fashionable for them to want straight hair. Long European hair was woven to their own short, tight curls. At this very moment, two of our girls are in New York learning the technique, and when they return they will be sent to all our European centres to teach the method to your own operators. Then, when training is complete, we shall have a huge advertising campaign, which will cost me and Merv a packet, so it is up to you to make sure that your salesmen know how to sell a hair weave. Any questions?'

'Does it hurt?' said Helmut Kleiber from Frankfurt.

'Not at all', said Mervyn.

'Provided you have a reasonably high threshold', said Arnold.

Our thoughtful Spanish manager, José Maria Gonzales, said, 'If the base is tied to the client's own hair, what will happen when his hair grows? Will not the base become loose?'

'It will, José, indeed it will', said Arnold.

'That is very bad, sir', said Kleiber. 'I thought there was an imper- fection with this weaving. It seemed too good.'

'It is good, Helmut, you old pessimist', said Arnold. 'Listen, you sell a hair weave for, say, two thousand marks, and after two months it becomes loose, so your client has to return for a tightening of the base, for which you charge seventy-five marks. As long as he wears the hair weave, he will return every two months for tightenings, so you have an additional regular income.'

'*Magnifique*', sighed Jean-Paul Jacquier from Paris. 'Surely it was a French idea?'

There was a knock at the door and the receptionist ushered in a trendy young man, whom Arnold introduced as our advertising account executive. 'Bernie has some new ideas for our campaign', Arnold said. 'Let's see them, Bernie.'

The young man produced some rough sketches from his folder. The first one showed a handsome, virile and hirsute man lying in bed next to a young lady. The second one showed the same man sitting up in bed, hair attractively tousled, with his friend lying by his side looking dreamy. The third showed them standing together, deshabille, the lady running her hand through her partner's hair. The copy suggested that a hair weave was indistinguishable from real hair.

'These are useless, Bernie', said Arnold. 'We all know that sex is the reason for men wearing wigs, but these are in bad taste.'

'Steady on, Mr Peaman', said Bernie. 'If you look at the girl, you will notice that she is wearing a wedding ring.'

'Ah,' said Jean-Paul, 'what British innocence. Whose wife is she, eh?'

'The point is', said Arnold, 'that these are so unsubtle. A sensitive man would be put off a hair weave because his friends would think that he wanted it for sexual reasons, and they would laugh at him.'

'Why should they laugh?' said a puzzled Signor Baroni. 'Of course that is the reason. No Italian man would laugh, my friends. He would admire.'

'Let me explain', said Arnold. 'We want an advertisement that pictures a man playing football, or golf, or driving an open car, fast, with a girl by his side. Our advertisement would appear to say, "If you have a hair weave you can indulge in healthy activity of all kinds, and no one will ever know that you are really as bald as a coot." But what we are actually saying, and our potential client will sense it, is, "With a hair weave you can make love without your wig dropping off on the pillow." '

Bernie took notes, and went back to the drawing-board.

'Finally,' said Arnold, 'we must discuss the name that we shall call our hair weaving. It must be a word acceptable to all countries. I prefer not to use an English name. Any suggestions?'

There were many suggestions, and an equal number of objections. Chauvinism was rife, and ancient prejudices were aired, and the atmosphere became similar to any United Nations peace commission. Bernie, who had returned, having forgotten his folder, said, 'My wife is Swedish. She could suggest a Swedish word. Does anyone have any objections?'

Amazingly, nobody did. Sweden is a country which arouses no antipathy amongst its European neighbours (except, as I later discovered, the Danes, who know the Swedes best).

'What was your wife's maiden name?' asked Mervyn.

'Lundqvist', said Bernie.

'That's it, then', said Mervyn. 'We will call it 'The Lundqvist System of Hair Weaving.' And everyone agreed, because Mervyn was the boss.

125

Methods of Despatch. The Alternative to CIF and FOB in Export Deliveries

'When are you returning to Holland?' asked Arnold.

'In a couple of days', I said.

'Call and see us before you go', Arnold said. 'I'd like you to take some True-Top wigs back. There is a big delivery due tomorrow, and if we post them we may get caught for customs duty.'

'Are you asking me to smuggle wigs into Holland?' I asked.

'Sure', Mervyn said. 'We do it all the time. There's no danger of being caught. They never open cases at Schiphol, unless you're a hippie or Chinese.'

All night I worried about it. It was not so much that I should be damaging the Dutch economy, but it was the idea of having my case opened and searched, with the customs officer producing one by one, held by thumb and finger tip, contraband wigs, in front of all those people. A man's wig is entirely devoid of glamour and is, let's face it, an object of fun and derision. A glance at the Sunday newspapers surely illustrates where wigs stand in the glamour stakes: there is the wig advertisement, sandwiched between the cure for painful piles and the instrument for cutting off hard skin.

Against all my better judgement, I called at the office the next day to pick up the wigs. I was dismayed to find over twenty of them, far too many to hide in my shoes or sponge-bag, so I decided to secrete them about my person instead of putting them in my suitcase. I put one in each pocket, but apart from looking the very prototype of a man smuggling wigs, I was left with nine hair-pieces with no home, so I had to think again, and this time I found the perfect answer. I took a long piece of string and I tied a wig every six inches along its length. I undressed, and wound the string round my body. I looked like a Red Indian chief with an enviable collection of scalps, and in the secrecy of my room I did a realistic war dance. Then I put my clothes on, with a struggle, and became at once a chubby business-man. Full of confidence, I made my way to London Airport, where I boarded an Amsterdam-bound DC8.

It was not a comfortable journey. I perspired so freely that the hostess kept bringing me cold drinks, but I became hotter and hotter in my hairy undergarment. Then I began to itch. My neighbour in the window seat looked at me askance as I scratched ceaselessly. Then he began to scratch, and we sat, scratching together, until he changed his seat, giving me a look of extreme distaste in passing.

Eventually, I waddled off to the toilet, where I bathed my steaming head, and unbuttoned all my clothes, flapping my arms to get some air circulating. Finally, feeling better, I did myself up and walked

126

back towards my seat, but the hostesses had their trolley out collecting coffee cups, and I had to squeeze between the trolley and a middle-aged lady in a gangway seat. She looked at me and gasped. It was a gasp of utter disgust, a sound I was becoming accustomed to, and I looked down and gave my own gasp of disgust. There was a thick hank of curly grey hair sticking out of my trouser zip. Covering it with both hands, I rushed back to the toilet, watched with interest by the hostesses and many of my fellow travellers. In the toilet I tugged at my zip, but it was stuck fast, and then the little metal tab came off in my hand. I was as near despair as I have ever been. Emergencies like this produce superhuman brain power, and I burned the hair from the front of my trousers with my cigarette lighter. The smell was appalling and I charred my suit, but at least I was fit for human company again, although the lady who followed me into the toilet did not think so, because she complained to the steward, who spent the remainder of the flight watching me coldly.

The forty-minute flight to Amsterdam lasted as long as the Kon-Tiki expedition, but we were finally deposited in the large antiseptic arrivals hall at Schiphol, and I quickly made my way towards the passport barrier. My heart stopped with fear when I felt a dragging sensation at my foot, and I looked behind me and saw the end of my piece of string, with two wigs attached, trailing on the floor. I shoved my hand down the front of my trousers and pulled the string hard, dragging the wigs back to safety. This action was accompanied by an ear-piercing shriek from a woman out of my vision, and I hurried on. The shrieking continued, and I heard the sound of running feet, and my shoulder was grasped. It was an American touring grandmother.

'Two rats have just run up your trouser leg', she panted.

'Nonsense', I said.

'But they have, I saw them. Two great big rats, a brown one and a black one. Whoosh, right up, they went!'

'Madam,' I said, 'if two rats had run up my leg, I would be the first to know.'

We were joined by an elderly, limping man, also an American.

'Son,' he said, 'forgive my intrusion, but a couple of gophers just shot up your leg. They can be a dangerous beast in a guy's pants. Just thought I'd tell you.'

'How did you know they were golfers?', I hissed. 'Were they carrying putters?'

'Anyway, they were rats,' the lady said, 'and if this young fella doesn't do something real fast, they'll do him an injury he'll regret.'

The small crowd around us parted to let through an airport official. In growing bewilderment he listened to the Americans.

127

'Are you aware, sir,' he said, 'of the strict regulations concerning the importation of animals into Holland?'

'There are no animals', I protested. 'It must have been an optical illusion or something. Look!' I said, standing astride. 'Can you see anything moving?'

Everyone studied my legs. 'Your trousers are burnt, sir', the official said.

'I dropped a cigarette in my lap', I lied.

'I guess it was an illusion', the old man said. 'My eyes ain't too good nowadays. Sorry, son.'

The lady said, 'If you find anything when you get to your hotel, let me know, willya? Here's my card. I'm staying at the Krasnapolsky.'

I promised her that I would examine the contents of my trousers as soon as possible and inform her if any livestock were present. Then, without a qualm, as though having been through fire and emerged purged, I sailed past passport control and customs.

Outside the airport an Englishman spoke to me. I recognised him from the plane.

'I don't know what you have in your trousers,' he said, 'but I would like to thank you for a most entertaining journey.'

Back at my flat, I undressed and took a long, cool shower. The wigs seemed none the worse, except for the one I had burned. Then the telephone rang, and it was Arnold.

'Get through all right? Good, I told you so. It's a piece of cake.'

'It's a piece of something,' I said, 'but it certainly isn't cake.'

Critical Decision Analysis Applied to Simulated Origins

The Atomic Reading press conference was due to start at midday, and everything was well rehearsed. Our public relations officer had promised us a good attendance by the Dutch Press, and all our staff were waiting nervously at our institute in the Kaizergracht, sampling the alcoholic refreshments that are essential, so the PRO said, to a successful meeting with the press. Expensive brochures had been produced, full of information which Bob Bishop had given us concerning the way Atomic Reading had been accepted by most of the world's educational authorities. Three of our successful students were present, ready to give demonstrations of their phenomenal reading speeds, but I was disappointed by the absence of the four whom I had specially asked to attend: the youngest, the oldest, the most beautiful, and the most brilliant, the ones that the press could really have got their teeth into. The parents of our youngest, a bright fourteen-year-old, would not allow their daughter to be the subject of nationwide publicity, unless they were paid 2,500 guilders. The

128

oldest was forbidden to attend by his doctor on the grounds that the excitement might kill him. The beautiful Miss Ellie Mientjes was pregnant, it was rumoured, by one of our instructors, and the brilliant Pieter van Poll was suffering from a nervous breakdown.

At eleven fifteen two men appeared at reception and demanded to see the principal, and Mr Klein led them into his office. Five minutes later, grey-faced, he sent for me. His visitors were internationalites, bronzed, well-dressed, with a discreet flash of gold each time they moved. It was impossible to determine their nationality, for they were the new breed of men who swept effortlessly from one language to another, and their English, while fluent, was tinged with American, with Gallic undertones.

The spokesman, a tall man with a thin moustache, said, 'I understand, sir, that you are the personal representative of Mr Robert Bishop, and therefore control the activities of the so-called Atomic Reading Institutes of the Nederlands.'

'Yes', I said.

'In that case, I must ask you to cancel your press conference.'

'Impossible', I said.

'Then my associates and I will ruin it', he said.

'I see', I said. 'Well, you have put your case clearly, and now I suggest you leave or I shall ask Mr Klein to throw you out.'

No one moved. 'Mr Klein,' I said, 'throw these gentlemen out.'

Mr Klein said, 'I hurt my leg yesterday in the garden.'

'You haven't got a garden, Mr Klein', I said. 'You live on the seventh floor of an apartment block', but my initiative was lost. It was easy to see that Mr Klein was not British.

'Who are you?' I asked the strangers.

'My name is Rene Muller', the tall man said, handing me a card. 'I am president of the European division of Reading Atomics.'

I was incensed. 'You will never get away with this', I shouted. 'I shall see my lawyers immediately. This is blatant plagiarism. Mr Bishop will be furious.'

'He certainly will be,' said Muller, 'and may I compliment you on your choice of words. "Plagiarism" is exactly right.' He whispered to his companion, and then said, 'I suppose it is possible that you are unaware of the true situation. Would you please tell me your version of the origins of Atomic Reading?'

'I am not obliged to tell you anything,' I said, 'but I can spare you just five minutes. After a lifetime of study, Mr Bishop, a Harvard graduate, perfected a method of speed reading far in advance of any other system. He then formed a company, Atomic Reading, to spread this invaluable knowledge throughout the world. I am proud to be associated with him, and I deplore attempts by the unscrupulous to cash in on his success, and steal the results of his years of research.'

'Thank you', said Muller. 'One more question. How old is the company, Atomic Reading?'

'I am not certain', I said. 'Two years, perhaps even three.'

'What would you say', said Muller, 'if I proved to you, which I can, that my company, the Institute of Reading Atomics, was formed in the United States in the year 1950?'

I tried to think of something to say. 'Good heavens!' I said.

'And', went on Muller, 'that we are part of a highly respected multimillion-dollar organisation specialising in educational and recreational activity, for which Mr Bishop once worked, briefly, as a publicist and promotional assistant?'

'My goodness!' I said.

'Furthermore,' said Muller, 'your Atomic Reading instruction manual is identical to our Reading Atomics manual. Here, look for yourself', he said, passing to me two books. I studied them carefully.

'Yours is printed better,' I admitted, 'but ours is a nicer colour.'

'The Institute of Reading Atomics have schools throughout the Americas,' said Mr Muller, 'and this year intends to commence operations in Europe. I am in charge of the European theatre, and my assistant here is a vice-president, controlling Benelux. It is obvious to us that Mr Bishop, learning of our plans, decided to beat us into Europe by establishing as many schools as possible, with the object of blackmailing us into buying him out at an exhorbitant figure. This we will not do, you can tell Mr Bishop. We would be interested, however, in offering you two gentlemen important positions within our company. This depends on you cancelling your press conference today, and meeting the press later at our own conference.'

'Are you trying to bribe us, Mr Muller?' I asked, shock written all over my face.

'Yes, are you?' said Mr Klein, leaning forward eagerly. 'How much. . . .'

'Mr Klein and I are horrified', I said. 'Now get out, before Mr Klein loses his temper.'

'You will regret it', said Muller as he left.

Our PRO put his head round the door. 'The press are arriving', he said. 'Come and meet them, meneer Klein.'

Mr Klein had lost his enthusiasm, but I slapped his shoulder and said, 'Go out and slay 'em, Kleiney. I'm sure Mr Bishop can explain everything.'

As soon as Klein had gone, I telephoned Bob Bishop in London and told him all that had happened. 'Is it true, Bob?' I said.

'What do you think, Gordon?' he said. 'You know me, does it sound like the sort of stroke I would pull?'

I thought hard and long. 'Actually, Bob, yes, it does', I said.

'Well, there you are then. What are you worrying about. They can't touch us, take my word for it. Just get us a good press conference today, and you'll start to make yourself some real money.'

'What about my contract?' I asked him.

'I had it yesterday,' he said, 'but I noticed that there was a clause in it that seemed a bit unfair to you, so I sent it back to the lawyers for revision. Don't you worry, old Bob'll take care of you.'

I put the phone down, not completely happy.

The Fourth Estate and its Usefulness in Commercial and Educational Promotion

The press conference was not entirely successful. The demonstrations were impressive, and Mr Klein's speech was a *tour de force*, but some of the reporters had obviously been briefed by Mr Muller, and began to ask questions about Reading Atomics. Klein was quite unable to deal with the uproar when the pressmen found that they were on to a scandal, and the resultant publicity in the Dutch newspapers, while all that we could have desired spacewise, gave me little joy contents-wise.

'Atomic Reading *v.* Reading Atomics', headed two columns in the *Amsterdamse Courant*. 'Educational Espionage Alleged', blared the *Haagsche Dagblad*. The cartoonist in the *Algemeen Nieuwsblad* showed our symbol of an eye within an eye being punched by a fist within a fist.

Far more painful, however, were the first writs received a week after the press conference, and the subsequent hearings at courts in The Hague and Cologne, where we lost the right to use the name Atomic Reading.

We struggled on, but income dropped and legal charges increased, and accounts and wages were unpaid so I flew to London to face Bob Bishop with our problems and to demand a substantial transfer of funds.

Patrick Coogan, the accountant, was the only occupant of the Atomic Reading Institute in Bloomsbury. He was sitting in his shirt-sleeves at his desk, and he smiled wearily.

'What's happened, Patrick?' I said. 'Where is everybody?'

'"Tis a long story,' he said, 'but I'll shorten it for you. We are bust, my friend. Broke.'

'How much?' I asked.

'I haven't finished going through the books,' Patrick said, 'but it looks like £120,000.'

'Assets?' I asked.

'Nil.'

'Where's Bob?'

'Gone.'

'Where?'

'I don't know. Two days ago he vanished. His flat is empty.'

'No messages?'

'Nary a word', Patrick said. 'Oh yes, he left this for you.'

He handed me an envelope with my name on it, I tore it open. It was my contract.

Chapter 12

The Growth Reversal Method of Overhead Reduction

Business at the Mervarn hair clinics was brisk enough to reassure me that my consultancy brief was good for many a year to come. One small cloud on the horizon was the unwillingness of a certain meneer Wanmakers to accept the fact that he had been well and truly taken for 5,640 guilders, and had his hair not finally given up the unequal struggle of trying to survive two years of Mervarn's potions and unguents, he would still be paying happily for the privilege of keeping Arnold Peaman and Mervyn Flank in velvet collared Crombies.

Meneer Wanmakers wanted his money back.

In vain were Hans Pranger's protestations that such a demand offended against the very foundations of the Mervarn organisation. Meneer Wanmakers should understand, said Hans, that without the Mervarn treatment his hair would have lasted only one year instead of two. Furthermore, although meneer Wanmakers's hair had finally died on him, it had died clean.

Meneer Wanmakers uttered threats, and that was when I was called in. A meeting was arranged, and I met the protagonist, who had brought a companion, a silent young woman who took copious notes.

'You have no legal right to have your payments refunded', I told meneer Wanmakers, 'despite the failure of our desperate attempts to save your hair. Does a doctor return his fees', I asked cleverly, 'if his patient dies after two years of devoted treatment?'

Meneer Wanmakers did not understand English, and Hans Pranger repeated my comments in Dutch. They must have lost something in the translation, because meneer Wanmakers stood up and grabbed my throat.

I tried again. 'You think our charges were excessive, but you must not relate them to the intrinsic value of the preparations used on your head, or the amount of electricity consumed during high frequency treatment. You are paying for expertise, for meneer Pranger's long years of training, and for our colossal research expenses.'

Hans translated, hesitantly, and this time meneer Wanmakers launched into a flood of what sounded like abuse, but since all Dutch sounded like abuse to me, I assumed that he was putting forward his

133

reasoned answer to my statement, perhaps even apologising. But I was wrong. It was abuse.

'Nothing will change his mind', Hans said. 'Unless he gets back his money, he will cause trouble.'

'Then there is no point in continuing our conversation', I said. '*Tot zien, meneer Wanmakers, goed middag, mevrouw*', and I left the room, hoping that my use of their native tongue would mollify them.

Later, when they had gone, I said to Hans, 'He won't do anything to make himself look ridiculous in the eyes of the public. Bald men are far too sensitive, luckily for us. You won't hear another word from Wanmakers, believe me.'

Pandora, Holland's largest-circulation magazine, was a publication for which I had a lot of respect. I used it occasionally for advertising True-Top wigs, and although it had a reputation for muck-raking, what popular magazine doesn't? The pictures were always excellent, even if I was unable to understand the accompanying comments, but no caption was necessary for the large photograph which headed the next month's leading feature. There was meneer Wanmakers, his bald head reflecting the camera flash, his left hand holding his nose, and his right hand pouring a clearly labelled bottle of Mervarn shampoo into a WC pan. I could also understand the title of the article: My bald head cost me 5,640 guilders.

I jumped into a taxi and went to our advertising agency. Joop Baggers, who dealt with the Mervarn account, met me at the door. We waved our copies of Pandora at each other.

'This is terrible, Joop', I said. 'You must translate it for me. I can only understand the heading.'

'It gets worse', Joop said gloomily.

Pandora had done a good job. The beginning of the four-page article dealt with Wanmakers's experiences at the clinic, two years of examinations, where he was invariably assured that his hair was becoming stronger. 'The old weak hairs have to fall out before the new growth starts', was one of the excuses given to him when he complained that his hair was vanishing. 'Your hair is growing vigorously,' he was told on another occasion, 'but below the surface. Another course of treatment is required to soften the scalp, and then the new hair will burst through like spring grass.'

Then *Pandora*'s reporters gave the results of their research on our clinic managers, qualified trichologists all. Hans Pranger of Amsterdam, it was revealed, was a shoe salesman until his two-week crash course in London. De Vries, of The Hague, was a student of economics until he tried a little experimenting with the economics of the Dutch giro system, thus becoming a guest of Her Majesty Queen Juliana for a two-year period. It was during his six months' remission for good behaviour that he became a hair expert. Kerkhof of Rotter-dam had sold encyclopedias to the American forces in Germany, and Verhoeven of Utrecht had been a barman in Breda.

Finally, *Pandora* had analysed Mervarn's special shampoos, hair conditioners, anti-dandruff lotions and all the other wonder mixtures, and found them wanting. The shampoo was identical in make-up to a well-known washing-up liquid, but heavily diluted, and the remainder were unexceptional in all but price.

'What can we do about it?' I asked Joop Baggers. 'Can we sue?'

'Better', said Joop, 'that we should pray.'

The week's taking at the four Mervarn hair clinics in Holland dropped from the average 35,000 guilders to 107 guilders. We were informed that the Dutch Advertising Commission had forbidden all publications to accept further advertisements for Mervarn, who moved swiftly and efficiently into liquidation. *Pandora* was widely distributed in Belgium, and our Brussels clinic also closed. The Germans took up the story, and closed the clinics in Hamburg, Bremen and Hanover.

I met Arnold Peaman and Mervyn Flank in Paris, where they felt safe. They were philosophical. 'Easy come. . . .' said Mervyn.

'We made a lot of money', said Arnold.

'If only you had given Wanmakers his money back', mused Mervyn.

'What would you have done?' I asked.

'We would have fired you', said Arnold.

The Making of a Campaign. Group Fulfilment and Activity Enrichment in Merit Promotion

With a thunderous discharge of advertising expenditure, the Lundqvist System of Hair Weaving burst upon the balding world. Simultaneously in France, Belgium, Holland, Germany and Spain, True-Top announced the greatest boon to mankind since the mini-skirt. In Italy, the newspapers were on strike.

'Sensational News from America!' blared our advertisements, showing a gentleman washing his hair vigorously. 'Not a wig, not a transplant, not a skin graft, but an entirely new method of replacing your lost hair painlessly and permanently! Write or telephone NOW to your nearest True-Top centre!'

For three days our telephones rang almost ceaselessly. Salesmen were delirious with delight at the thought of their commission to come, and managers beamed at the prospect of huge bonuses. Only the operators, young girls mostly between the ages of seventeen and twenty-two, failed to share in the general feeling of euphoria because they were the ones who had to make the hair weaves, and they were unsure of their expertise, having had too short a training and very little practice. I assured them all, as I made a lightning tour of our branches, that everything would be all right on the day. In England, I told them, hair weaves were as common as haircuts, and thousands of contented clients swore by Lundqvist hair weaves. This was not 100 per cent true, because in fact at that particular moment in time only three hair weaves had been completed in England, all of which had flopped over their owners' ears within a few days. But I knew that this was no way to run a business, and that Arnold Peaman and Mervyn Flank would spare no expense to perfect their system in which so much money had been invested.

The very first client to have a hair weave in Holland was a young man called Vos. He was nervous, but not as nervous as Eta and Ellie, the two girls who were to perform the metamorphosis. On the other hand, three of us exuded confidence: Albert, who had sold the weave to Vos, Leo the hairdresser, whose only job was to wait until the weave was completed and then to cut and style it, and I, who had just collected eighteen hundred guilders in cash from our client. A room had been prepared for the weaving operation on the first floor of the True-Top shop, and as advised by London, we had removed the looking-glass from the wall. A client, we had been told, might well faint during the weaving process if he caught sight of his tortured scalp.

It was three o'clock on a sunny afternoon in Amsterdam when Vos sat down in the comfortable chair, Eta and Ellie on either side of him, to have his hair weave. Leo and I settled down for a quiet game of chess, while Albert poked away at his teeth with a dentist's probe. Albert always carried a complete set of dental tools in his breast pocket. He stole them from his dentist, his justification being that he was always overcharged. He offered to steal a set for me, but I told him not to bother.

At four thirty Leo checkmated me, so I went in to see how the hair weave was progressing. Vos was gripping the arms of his chair, and the girls were still trying to fasten the base to his head.

'Keep it up', I said cheerfully. 'There's plenty of time.'

I took Leo and Albert out for a drink, and at six o'clock Leo said, 'I must hurry back. They may be waiting for me.' But they were not waiting for Leo. They were waiting for inspiration, I think, because the base would not stay firm to Vos's head. The girls were pale and upset, and Vos had gone yellow, except for his scalp, which was red. The base, like a great spider's web, sat limply on the centre of his head.

'Why don't you rest for a while?' I said. 'Albert will make coffee, and Leo will fetch something to eat.'

136

'Please sir, I am not hungry,' Vos said in a low, cracked voice, 'but I would like a cold beer.'

'Anything', I said, handing Leo a hundred guilder note from the wad that Vos had given me. 'Get ten cold beers, Leo. It may be a long night.'

I went upstairs to my bedroom and telephoned Jean-Paul Jacquiere, the manager of True-Top, Paris.

'How did your first hair weave go, Jean-Paul?' I said.

'It lasted nine hours', he said. 'As soon as the client stood up, he fell down. He was taken to hospital, where they cut his weave off. The client demands a refund. What should I do?'

'What you must do', I said, 'is this.' Then I put the receiver down, as though I had been accidentally cut off. This was a case where nobody could win.

At seven o'clock I sent Albert out to work, with instructions to sell wigs, not weaves, and I ordered Leo to help the two girls, who were near despair. I went out to dinner, the thought uppermost in my mind being that Consultants must never become involved in physical work. After dinner I went to a cinema in the Rembrandt-splein, and saw a German film with Dutch sub-titles. Then I visited a bar and whiled away another hour, until I convinced myself that Vos's hair weave must have been satisfactorily completed. I returned to the shop, and saw that the lights were still on, so I crept upstairs to bed, refusing to become involved.

But I was involved. Vos was in my bed.

I rushed downstairs, and found the two girls and Leo in cheerful spirits, having almost emptied a bottle of *jonge genever*, Dutch gin.

'We all needed a break', Leo explained.

'How about giving me a break', I said. 'Why is Vos in my bed?'

'He drank all the beer', Ellie giggled. 'His hair weave is half finished.'

'Only half!' I said. 'It is past midnight. You have been working on him for hours.'

'His head is so painful', Eta explained. 'It is bleeding, too.'

She began to cry. Ellie began to cry. Leo began to cry.

'Quiet', I commanded. 'Why are you crying, Leo?'

'I had a date at eight o'clock', he said. 'He'll never speak to me again.'

'Listen', I told them. 'Get Vos out of bed and finish his weave. I'm going out again, and when I return in an hour I want you all gone.'

I wandered along to the Blue Note night club, and popped in to see the topless orchestra. Albert was there, sitting in a corner with a girl, and manicuring her nails with his dentist's tools. When he saw me he waved and jerked his head backwards so that his wig lifted off like a cap and hung behind his head. The girl screamed and ran off.

'I sold three weaves tonight', he said. 'Six thousand guilders. I earn nine hundred and fifty. I'll buy you a drink.'

'I told you not to sell weaves', I said. 'They can't do them properly yet.'

'That's not my affair', he said. 'I have to sell them, they have to make them.'

At three o'clock in the morning Albert and I went back to the shop. Vos was asleep in his chair, and the girls, looking like death, were performing the final touches to his weave. It looked terrible. We woke Vos up, and Leo styled his new hair. Then he put a pen in his hand and asked him to sign a certificate of satisfaction. Vos signed shakily. At half past three everybody left and I went to bed, cursing the Lundqvist System of Hair Weaving.

I was having an unpleasant dream, when I was aroused into an equally unpleasant reality. The front bell was ringing, and it was Vos. The time was seven o'clock.

'Take it off', he begged, as he lurched into the shop. 'I am desperate with the agonies in the head.'

'Why, Mr Vos,' I said, 'I can't do that. I am not allowed to interfere with the work of the True-Top technicians. Besides, I don't know how to take it off.'

'Cut it,' he said, 'pull it. Anything. The pain is unstandable.'

'But Mr Vos,' I stammered, terrified of touching his head, 'I only have my pyjamas on.'

'I forgive you for not dressing', he said. 'Afterwards, then you can dress.'

We went upstairs to the weaving-room, and I picked up a pair of scissors. 'What about your certificate of satisfaction?' I asked. 'You signed it only four hours ago.'

He broke into a stream of forceful Dutch, of which I understood not a word, but it seemed to be instructions for the disposal of the certificate.

'I am not authorised to refund your money', I said.

'Keep the money', he said.

'But I shall arrange for a new hair weaving for you as soon as possible.'

'No!' he shouted. 'Not that. Another two thousand guilders I shall give you not to have another hair weave.'

I cut off his hair weave. It was the bravest thing I have ever done. His scalp was raw, but Vos was happy. I made a pot of tea for two, and we sat and chatted about unemployment in the mining area of

Limburg. Then Vos went home, and I went back to bed, pondering on the total lack of solid achievement during the past eighteen hours.

Selective Use of Television for Optimum Results, and the Advance-Reversal Assessment. The Automatic Close Technique

Our hair weaves became better over the next few weeks. We cut the time from Vos's twelve and a half hours to two and a half, and with practice the operation became virtually painless. Business flourished, and I basked in the reflected glory of doubled and trebled turnovers as I jetted from city to city. Customs officials began to recognise me, and air hostesses greeted me by name, the ultimate accolade for the international traveller.

It did not last. Arnold Peaman and Mervyn Flank began to dispose of their continental businesses. True-Top Italy and Spain were sold for tremendous sums, and in Paris, where rents had become astronomical and taxes prohibitive, the business was transferred to the French manager who knew, as do all Frenchmen, how to deal with the tax collector. Then Germany and Switzerland were sold, and my activities were confined to Holland and Belgium. I was not unduly disturbed, because we were growing so rapidly that my time was fully occupied, and Arnold assured me that there would be no more selling.

A bulky letter arrived at the Amsterdam office one morning, addressed to the director. I opened it, and saw with some excitement that it was from a television company in Hilversum, so I gave it to my secretary to translate. She paled as she read it.

'It's from Keizer Consumentie, Mr Bennett', she said.

'They want us to advertise on television?' I said. 'It's worth considering.'

'No', she said. 'It means "the consumer is emperor". It is a very powerful consumer protection programme. Terrible people', she added to put me at my ease.

'What do they want?' I said. 'We shall naturally help them all we can.'

'They never want help', she said. 'Only trouble. When people have complaints about firms, they write to Keizer Consumentie, who make a wicked programme and try to close down the firm.'

'Surely,' I said, 'you are not telling me that someone has complained about True-Top?'

'Not exactly "someone". There are photocopies of . . .' she began counting, 'thirty-eight letters of complaint. The producer wants us to give our answers to these complaints.'

'Read out the complaints', I said, feeling the old familiar stone in the pit of the stomach.

'Meneer de Haan writes, "The first time I wore my 1,500 guilder wig from True-Top, the wind blew it into the North Sea." '

'Well, that's not a valid complaint', I said. 'The wind on the coast would blow your head into the North Sea. He couldn't have fixed it on properly. What's the next complaint?'

'From meneer Roodenburg. "My hair weave from True-Top cost me 1,755 guilders. From the first it gave me great pain. When I comb it, plucks stayed behind in the comb." '

'Plucks?' I said. 'Surely not.'

' "Gradually, strings of the mat got loose, and it fell over my eyes in the street." '

'Next', I said wearily.

'Meneer van Blonk says, "My hair weave after five days got loose. Very carefully I took a shower and in no time the hair was one inextricable clew." '

'Inextricable clew?' I echoed. 'What is a clew?'

'I don't know the English word', she said.

'Never mind', I told her. 'I think I know.'

'Do you want more?' she said. 'It is very distressful. Here, meneer Smoes talks of his weave: "At the slightest sigh of wind, the hair stood to all directions. I walked for a monkey in the street, and whole plucks of hair got loose." '

'Enough!' I said. 'Tell me, is Keizer Consumentie a popular programme?'

'Not with firms', she said.

'I believe you', I said. 'What about the viewing public?'

'They understand that it is a strong, cruel programme, very unfair sometimes, and making many firms bankrupt.'

'So the Dutch, being a fair-minded, civilised people, refuse to watch it?'

'No', she said. 'Everybody watches it.'

'Get me the producer on the telephone', I said.

Meneer Behage spoke good English, and was polite but not warm.

'Do you intend to feature my firm on your programme?' I asked.

'Perhaps', he said. 'It is not our policy to reveal advance details of Keizer Consumentie.'

'What opportunities shall we have to answer your charges, assuming we are featured?'

'You can comment on the letters of complaint that we sent you.'

'Is that all?' I said. 'Can we not prepare a proper defence? Thirty-eight letters of complaint is not a lot compared to our thousands of satisfied customers.'

'We are not interested in satisfied customers, Mr Bennett', he said. 'It is up to you to publicise your successes at your own cost. We deal with the individual who has no other way of expressing his grievance than to tell us about it. If we feel that the grievance is justified, we tell the consumers of Holland.'

'So,' I said, 'you refuse to tell me if, or when, you intend to destroy my company. You refuse to allow me to defend myself. You are not concerned at the prospect of putting many people out of work. How can this happen in a democratic country?'

'Keizer Consumentie has nothing to do with politics, Mr Bennett', he said. 'Our only interest is the protection of the Dutch consumer.'

That ended our conversation. I replied to all the letters of complaint, but I knew we had no chance.

Albert and I watched the programme together. True-Top was torn asunder. Ten of our old clients appeared, my letter of explanation was not mentioned, and I half expected to see a lynching party advancing along Kalvestraat.

Our next advertisement, a full page costing fourteen thousand guilders, brought us four coupons, all abusive. However, our volume of mail remained steady, bolstered by letters from lawyers demanding the return of clients' money, and cancellations from all parts of Holland and Belgium.

Once again I met Arnold Peaman and Mervyn Flank, this time in neutral Copenhagen. They were, as usual, unruffled.

'You can understand it', Arnold said. 'These Dutchmen, who kid themselves that they are the world's toughest businessmen, see a couple of Englishmen walk in and take over an entire industry from under their noses. Naturally they resent it.'

'At least', I said, 'I have nothing to reproach myself for. No Consultant could have done more to build True-Top, and I can't think of anything I might have done to prevent the ultimate disaster. What more can I say?'

'How about', suggested Mervyn, ' "Goodbye"?'

Albert and I were talking in my small hotel, where I had moved when the True-Top shop closed down.

'This is the end', he said. 'I'm the world's greatest wig salesman with no wigs to sell, and you are a Management Consultant with nothing to management consult about. I think I'll go back to Australia. We are finished in this country, my friend.'

'Finished?' I said. 'We're just starting. Listen. . . .'

THE GORDON BENNETT SCHOOL OF BUSINESS

(Incorporating The Albert Konig School of Salesmanship, The Gordon Bennett Common Market Academy of Management Consultancy, Supersonic Reading (Universal) Inc., World Wide Wigs, NV, The Euro Educational and Economic Kulturbund GmbH (EEEK), etc., etc.)

Never has the future held more promise for the man with initiative. Europe, bulging with prosperity, is at the mercy of the entrepreneur. The Gordon Bennett School of Business trains selected pupils to break into the ranks of the new breed of International Businessman.

Each year the Gordon Bennett School of Business releases into Golden Europe an infusion of wisdom-crammed, clear-eyed, quietly purposeful Supermen and women, who will all become rich before the end of the decade.

We produce tycoons, and a list of Old Gordon Bennett SOB's—which cannot be published, because of the strict code of ethics which guides our every move—would astonish the general public.

Our faculty includes men whose names are spoken with awe in their chosen field. Professor Albert Konig, co-principal of the school, is indisputably the world's greatest authority on the psychology of selling. Professor Klein, senior tutor, is the recognised master of speed reading and sex shops.

To reserve a place on our next course, complete the coupon below and return it AT ONCE with your initial registration fee of Ten Pounds (£10). For the convenience of students, this fee may be paid IN ANY RECOGNISED CURRENCY.

HURRY! Only a limited number of places are still available. Indecision is the hallmark of the failure!

DO NOT, UNDER ANY CIRCUMSTANCES, MAKE YOUR CHEQUE PAYABLE TO PROFESSOR ALBERT KONIG.

...............................cut here.....................................

To GBSOB. PO BOX 953/GB
I wish to take my first step to financial success with THE GORDON BENNETT SCHOOL OF BUSINESS. I ENCLOSE £10 REGISTRATION FEE which is not returnable.

NAME   AGE   SEX
ADDRESS
PRESENT OCCUPATION
FATHER'S OCCUPATION
FATHER'S STATE OF HEALTH
FATHER'S STATE OF HAIR

Amsterdam : Rotterdam: Paris: Strasbourg: Rome: Milan: Zurich: Brussels: Antwerp: Cologne: Frankfurt: London: Huddersfield